THE RICHEST PLACE
ON EARTH

The Story of Virginia City, Nevada, and the
Heyday of the Comstock Lode

THE RICHEST
PLACE
ON EARTH

The Story of Virginia City, Nevada, and the
Heyday of the Comstock Lode

WARREN HINCKLE

&

FREDRIC HOBBS

With drawings by FREDRIC HOBBS

Houghton Mifflin Company   Boston   1978

LIBRARY OF CONGRESS CATALOGING IN PUBLICATION DATA

Hinckle, Warren.

   The richest place on earth.
   1. Virginia City, Nev.—History.   2. Comstock Lode,
Nev.   I. Hobbs, Fredric, joint author.   II. Title.
F849.V8H56   979.3′56   77-11865
ISBN 0-395-25348-9

Printed in the United States of America

M 10 9 8 7 6 5 4 3 2 1

To
DAN DE QUILLE
AND
THE MUCKERS AND POWDER MONKEYS
OF THE COMSTOCK LODE

The young Mark Twain

Foreword

THE MAD ORGANIST
OF THE COMSTOCK

The late silver-spooned boulevardier Lucius Beebe, whose appreciation of the Irish in general was less than overwhelming but who curtsied to wealth in any robe, tells a story in *The Big Spenders* that captures the rash spirit of Virginia City in its boom days. Two Irish bonanza kings to be, John Mackay and his partner-in-muck, Jim Fair, trekked the 250 miles from San Francisco across the High Sierra to the windswept wasteland of the Comstock and came over the pass hungry and tired to behold below them the twenty-four-hour exercise in bacchanalia that was the mining town of Virginia City. Mackay reached in his pocket to find it empty and asked Fair if he had any money on him.

"Here's four bits; it's the only money I have in the world," Fair replied.

Mackay took the coin and sent it spinning into the Nevada sagebrush deep down the hillside.

"Whatever did you do that for, John?"

"So we can arrive like gentlemen."

When Mackay died some forty years later, his secretary told the press it was impossible to estimate his employer's fortune within $20 million. And Mackay's granddaughter married Irving Berlin.

Virginia City was once the richest place on earth. It has been as productive as a sucked egg since its silver mines petered out in the 1880s, but so fabulous were the fortunes produced and the manner of their spending and squandering so superlative that it burns through the fog of historical memory as a Cinderella city, a real-life, uniquely American Camelot devoted to the questionable art of conspicuous consumption. The Golconda from the deep mines of the Comstock changed the face of the West, enriched the North in the Civil War, built San Francisco into a Pacific Paris, laid the Atlantic cable, founded the Hearst newspaper empire, introduced Shanty Irish to the Court of St. James and the boudoirs of the Vanderbilts, spawned the first environmentalist, created frontier Medicis and uncommon Scrooges, and fattened the lean meat of the American dream with the carbohydrate of success stories about lumpen mining stock speculators who struck it rich—butter salesmen wandering around in morning coats and cleaning ladies scrubbing floors with diamond-encrusted hands.

Seventy-five years after all this had happened and Virginia City had become for all practical purposes save the collecting of tourists' pennies a ghost town, the aforementioned Lucius Beebe, oenophile and unrepentant Edwardian, chugged across the country in his private railroad car, puffed up the steep, winding, twenty-mile road separating Virginia City from the plastic of Reno and settled down in the mountain city for the rest of his unnatural life.

I knew Beebe when we were both writing for the *Chronicle*, San Francisco's daily funny paper. Beebe was as snobbish as a pewter pitcher of martinis and as brittle as a frozen Hershey bar. A woman came up to him at a cocktail party and complained about some department of the *Chronicle*. Beebe slapped her with his eyes. "Madam," he said, "I write for the *Chronicle* but I never *read* it."

Beebe had foaled café society in an acidulously snobbish column in which he covered the upper classes for the New York *Herald Tribune*. Beebe was one of their number but in the words of Hilaire Belloc, "Like many of the upper class, he loved the sound of smashing glass." He played high stakes cat's cradle in the thirties and forties in the velvet bomb shelters of 21 and Morocco, the Turkish baths of the Biltmore, and the magnificent zoo of Bleeck's Artists and Writers Restaurant (formerly Club), a hard-drinking newspaper joint where the great and the demented took daily communion. At Bleeck's a daft barkeep scattered cracked corn to an imaginary flock of chickens behind the ice bins while Stanley Walker, the *Herald Tribune*'s great city editor, proclaimed cirrhosis of the liver as the occupational disease of the journalist, and Gene Fowler, the biographer of John Barrymore, announced that money is for throwing off the back of trains. A constant ornament of existence in the expensive watering holes of Manhattan, Beebe became known from Antoine's in New Orleans to Loch-Ober's in Boston as "Mr. New York" (Walter Winchell called him "Lucious Lucius"), and his lordly walking around was so conspicuous that one critic described him as "a sort of sandwich board for the rich."

It was therefore an object of considerable consternation among the well-to-do when Beebe in 1950 pulled up stakes in New York with the abruptness of a vampire vanishing at dawn and moved to Virginia City, Nevada. Few could understand why. There was some speculation that it was due to Beebe's oft-stated belief that one should leave a party while it was still good. The fact was that Beebe had at last found a town worthy of his excesses. When Lucius went to bed at night he knelt to pray that the twentieth century, which he considered a "street accident," would go away before he waked. The wooden-boardwalked, Old West mountain city of Virginia contributed little to the distinction between fantasies and reality, and there Beebe was able to act out a life of nineteenth-century manners, amorality, distinguished letters, alcoholism, and howling personal journalism of the day of the code duello. Beebe walked around town in a claw-hammer coat and a wide brimmed black hat and the natives never gave him a second glance.

Western historian Oscar Lewis once said Nevada was "the wishing well of the nation." People come to Nevada from the forty-nine other states to pitch their pennies in the three-eyed fountains of Las Vegas and Reno and await the clatter of coins that substitutes for their dreams coming true. Lucius Beebe's dream of the good life in the amiable tradition of Nero materialized in the thin mountain air 6000 feet above Reno. He delighted in the fact that Virginia City maintained twenty saloons—that with only 650 men, women, and children in town. Lest the pinched-face statisticians of Alcoholics Anonymous find such numbers inexplicable, it should be explained that the fifties, despite the club-footed attempts of social historians to paint them a uniform gray, were actually fun-loving years for the middle classes and those salmon inclined toward frolic would stream uphill from Tahoe and Reno to Virginia City and environs where prostitution and most anything else was legal. The Comstock natives, a tough eggs-and-Tabasco sauce lot, minded their own business and expected visitors to follow their example. The confiscatory personal income tax is unknown in Nevada, and the state in Beebe's time, and now, remains uniquely the last wide-open space in the United States, a combination of Old West individualism and turn-of-the-century Southern California entrepreneurism. Nevada enshrined gambling and made divorce a family business; the Sagebrush State legalized acupuncture when it was still a Chinese word, and recently approved a fountain-of-youth drug, gerovital, which is as popular in Europe as Lydia Pinkham's but barred elsewhere in the U.S. by the Food and Drug Administration; and Nevada *loved* Laetrile.

In this citadel of anything goes, Beebe lived out his last fifteen years in a condition of life that the legendary *Harper's Bazaar* editor Henry Sell described as "expensive cheerfulness," which was, for all its ostentation, productive. Beebe with his partner and lifetime companion, Chuck Clegg, cranked out an impressive string of books on Western Americana in which they indulged an unbridled love affair with the train. As railroad historians, Bebbe and Clegg did for the High Iron what Macaulay did for the Whigs, and when they departed Virginia City during the inclement months they traveled about in a sultan's splendor in a private railway car named after the town and equipped with a fireplace, Turkish bath, and other voluptory amenities.

The visiting great—Cole Porter, restaurateur Dave Chasen, barrister Jake Ehrlich— would drop by Beebe and Clegg's Virginia City newspaper office to share the cup that cheers while throughout the country professors of journalism looked in horror on Beebe's magnificent resuscitation of the Virginia City *Territorial Enterprise*, the frontier newspaper where Mark Twain cut his editorial teeth. Beebe as publisher was a sort of Mad Organist of the Comstock, composing hydrophobic editorials against packaged breakfast cereals, digit dialing (Virginia City had crank-down phones), Billy Graham, zippers on men's pants, the American Newspaper Guild, woman's suffrage, TV dinners, the once-a-day mail delivery, the *Christian Science Monitor*, nuclear fission, Bobby Kennedy, one-ounce martinis, and the jet airplane—which the editorialist when he was in wine referred to as a "cartridge of death." These and other opinions were expressed at considerable length in Beebe's memorable form of the essay, which disdained periods and even semicolons, and exhibited even less regard for the paragraph.

Beebe's Baron Munchausen tastes notwithstanding, his newspaper was a classic of its kind, a black lotus late blooming out of the mud of barroom journalism. Its excessive tone was perfectly consistent with the history of Virginia City, which is in all facets a history of excess. During the bonanza decades on the Comstock, select horses had silver shoes, highwaymen gallantly treated their victims to champagne and truffles while they robbed them, and Mark Twain's *Enterprise* escalated the nineteenth-century journalistic tradition of crime hoaxes by publishing science-fiction hoaxes as news— by some accounts it was the first science fiction published in America.

The Comstock maintained a perverse balance sheet where every excess or debit deed had its positive side as an asset, recognized as such or not, of the times. The excesses of the *Enterprise* of the bonanza years gave birth to the laughter of genius. The excesses of Beebe's *Enterprise* served to remind one of what a dreary manufacturing business the news business has become. There was once in American journalism an adventurous sense of going down to the sea in ships, of doing business in great waters, and of course doing this under the influence of strong waters. Reporters used to spend as much time in the saloon as the city room, and the liveliness of journalism seems to have benefited from the general insobriety of the profession. The newshounding and -hening of greatness past combined wit and fortitude with unabashed rascality, the practical joke with the people's crusade. It was as forthright and natural as soldiers talking bawdy one moment and displaying great courage in battle the next. Beebe for a time picked up the warble of western journalism, individualistic, eccentric, and melodious even when off-key, which had reached its pitch during the forty years the Denver *Post* was run by Fred Bonfils and Harry Tammen like a three-ring circus, with the reporters kept in saloons and whorehouses until the ringmasters brought them on stage to perform. Bonfils and Tammen ruled the Rockies from a flaming red partner's room with a globe of the world and a shotgun on prominent display; in their wacky, cash-and-carry way they uncovered the Teapot Dome scandal and didn't even consider it a public service.

Such personal journalism is now, alas, one with the Kelvinator and the Edsel. Lucius Beebe in his salad days in the Virginia City *Territorial Enterprise* did one and all a favor by reminding us that journalists as well as mortals can be fools, but damn interesting ones.

One night during a fierce wind and rain storm on the Comstock, Lucius Beebe found Mr. T-Bone, his beloved Saint Bernard, staring intently into the storm as if trying to make out something in the dim distance. That night and for a week thereafter the Saint Bernard would not leave Beebe's side, following him everywhere. Beebe realized later that the dog was trying to tell him something: it was going to die. Mr. T-Bone died a week after the storm. Beebe wrote in his grief: "That night in the storm he heard a call from somewhere far off, something that only a dog could hear, and he sensed it on the storm wind that came down from the north where he had been born. A long, atavistic call from beyond the realm of senses and beyond his memory of puppyhood. He knew it then and wanted to tell me, and I never understood. It breaks my heart that I was so stupid and insensible."

Like many men who do not overly care for their fellow man, Lucius Beebe loved animals. He said that the huge Saint Bernard was one of the major forces in shaping his life, along with Jack Daniels whiskey and the *Herald Tribune* style book. When his dog died, Beebe wanted to die with it, to sit in eternity like the man and the dog in Thurber's famous drawing, facing west alone against the astral horizon of the stars, both no longer of this earth. Beebe and Clegg sold the *Enterprise* the year of Mr. T-Bone's death, in 1960. Without Beebe's pen the paper slowly sank back into the grave from whence he had resurrected it. Beebe continued to live part of the year in Virginia City until he died suddenly, of a heart attack, on February 4, 1966. Chuck Clegg attempted mouth-to-mouth resuscitation, but it was too late.

Wolcott Gibbs in a *New Yorker* profile of Beebe said that, in the words of the song popularized by Ethel Merman, "Beebe had class, with a capital K." Which is also to say, slightly crass class. The same epitaph could well be written for Virginia City. Every character in the spellbinding history of Virginia City overdid, in the direction of the outlandish. Virginia City's luck was of colossal proportions and so were its mistakes. It was never very good at being good, but when it was, it was very, very good, and when it was bad, it was so bad it was enchanting. The story of Virginia City could in many ways be taken as a brief for the Manichaean nature of man, or for the more commonplace observation about man's ability to do good and evil simultaneously.

Virginia City has always brought out the worst in people in a way that made it their best.

Warren Hinckle
San Francisco 1977

Contents

Part One

---◇---

THE BIG MAGNET

In the snowbound Sierra Nevada, during the perilous onrush of spring when land-slides are as common as crickets and the high mountain ravines become raging water-ways of melting snow, a solitary human figure made his way, walking ducklike across the deep drifts. A bulky canvas pouch slap-slapped against his back as his snowshoe-bound feet crunched into the powdered crust of the trail. These were alien sounds in a natural cathedral of sky-washed blue and green-tufted redwoods over a carpet of white where deer scrambled for footing.

There was frost on the man's beard and his eyelids beat like the wings of a humming-bird to keep the icy Sierra cold from hardening. His mouth puffed steam into the harsh bitter air with the regularity of a locomotive chimney moving through a tardy winter blizzard, blowing itself out into swirling clouds of snow. Snowshoe Thompson tight-ened the black knit cap around his long blond hair. His blue Viking eyes scouted for pitfalls ahead down the steep east slopes of the Sierra. He was the lone frontier post-man, delivering the overland mail from California to the isolated Washoe mining camps below, at the edge of the vast western desert.

A storm rolled down the mountain over the wilderness postman, leaving him wet and cold when he reached the floor of the Carson River valley. There was still a long walk ahead to the mining camps clinging to the stark stumpy hills of the diminutive Washoe mountain range. As a prelude to the great Sierra, the lowly Washoes were a Bach fugue before a Beethoven symphony.

The year was 1857. For the better part of a decade, weary, gold-lusting pioneers had pushed in mule teams and prairie schooners across the broad unsettled expanse of America toward the New Jerusalem of California. They had rejoiced at the sight of the wild and grim hills of the Washoe range—relief at last from the endless dust of the great plains and the stinging sand of the desert. Paying the briefest of respects to the Washoe, they hurriedly buried their dead and occasionally left the weak or un-

wanted behind in the valley. They pushed on, over the sun-struck Sierra, toward El Dorado on the other side.

Renegade Mormon settlers, failed adventurers, and Irish in flight from the potato famine formed the thin crust of humanity in the Washoe settlements—a strange breed of men and a few women who, for their own reasons, preferred to eke out an unrewarding existence in the shadow of the California rainbow rather than take the final step that might bring them to its legendary pot of gold. Many of their reasons for staying on in the grubby solitude of the windy hills were painfully personal, or perverse; but, for a large proportion of the Washoe colony, the motivations were more patent—these were the outcasts of El Dorado, the rejects and retards and unsuccessful bullies and outlaws who could find no place for themselves even in the unbridled California Gold Rush society. They slouched back across the Sierras to the first place they could find a grubstake or a scam.

It is to these rosinate citizens in that part of the Utah Territory, later known as Nevada, that Snowshoe Thompson faithfully delivered the United States mail—although there was little doubt that for many of them, no news would have been good news.

The frontier mailman, a stoic Norwegian, was not the type to volunteer his opinions. But climbing up the high rocky gorge known as Gold Cañon he wrinkled his broad nose in a solitary expression of displeasure. He had descended from a cathedral of nature to a level where the lower order of men had left its uninspiring mark. In its relentless passage to California, the Gold Rush throng had made bleaker one of God's original bleak places; the cottonwoods and scrub trees of Gold Cañon had been stripped from its boulder-strewn slopes; its creek ran rancid with effluvial matter; the grass was brown and stale like old straw. When the furious Washoe winds which gave the rustle of life to the desolate hills would regroup for a new blow, the stench of decay and death rose in the air—a grisly reminder of the hastily buried bodies of travelers who didn't make it beyond the desert, their remains scavenged by wolves and coyotes, their last resting places marked only by encircling buzzards.

A Mormon prospector, John Orr, passing through in 1850, had cut a gold nugget the size of a hazelnut out of a rocky pilaster at Devil's Gate, a narrow passage where the rocky walls of Gold Cañon almost touch, affording the canyon its grandiose name. Most prospectors took this blessed event not as a signal to dig further but to make haste across the Sierra—if there could be such a nugget in this forbidding place, what riches must await them in the vaunted clime of El Dorado!

"DEVIL'S GATE," 1857

Tens of thousands of fortune-seekers had since passed by Gold Cañon, scoffing at reports of its sparse and unusually flaky gold, which was always intermixed with blue black mud that made extracting the yellow metal a difficult and dirty process. This was nothing like the free and pure nuggets said to glitter like Christmas-tree ornaments on the golden riverbanks of California.

Yet certain remnants of humanity remained in the barren Washoe hills to fight the blue and black goo and extract its meager gold, and to these residents of "Johntown," as the main Gold Cañon mining settlement was called, Snowshoe Thompson dutifully made his seasonal mail run. As would any objective and intelligent observer, he too had cause to wonder why they hung on. Surely it wasn't money; the desert hills east of the Sierra had yielded barely $500,000 in gold since placer mining began there in the early 1850s; the average Gold Cañon prospector was lucky to fret out $2.00 a day—that in a community where flour cost $2.50 a sack.

There was a chill and a mystery about this shadowy place. The inhabitants seemed to be marking time, watching others pass them by, compelled to stay by some vague great expectation that the human tide flowing to California was missing something.

A clue to the mystery—if it could be called a mystery—lay in the massive rocky protuberance rising out of Gold Cañon to a peak some 7000 feet above the distant desert sands. Sun Mountain—so called because its peak caught the first rays of the rising sun—was the giant of the tiny Washoe range. A bony mountain of rock rising from sun-scorched hills scantily covered in gnarled sagebrush, it resembled an eroded desert pyramid. In the moonlit night the peak glowed with an unreal luminescence. By day, the direct desert sun washed out its few contrasts and character lines and the face of the tall, scarred rock suggested the eerie, stark texture of the moon.

To Snowshoe Thompson, snorting and puffing up the unsociable ravine, it seemed that this blasted brute rock somehow pulled the lost souls to this dissolute and forlorn place, although only the devil himself could guess its secret. The Piute Indians for centuries had called it the sundial of the desert. Snowshoe Thompson felt a similar sensation, an unseen force—like the pull of a big magnet.

The log cabin of Eilley Orrum was a rare symbol of hospitality, a hothouse rose of civilization in Gold Cañon. Eilley Orrum's role in the 99 percent male community was that of combination mother and sex object. A Scottish lassie of Highland origin, rumored to possess visionary qualities, she was a competent and businesslike woman who had her feet on the ground and who was confident of her charms. She did not blush if an admiring prospector was bold enough to describe her as "bonnie," and she absorbed compliments and dished out abuse with equal ease.

Eilley Orrum had shed two husbands, one of them a Mormon bishop in Salt Lake City. Settling in Gold Cañon, she had organized the domestic life of Johntown's tent-

and-shanty miners around the sturdy log cabin that she had built to her specifications. She took boarders but warned in advance that she did not "sleep" them. Her cabin was renowned for the meals of pork and beans she served each night to those citizens of Johntown with the price in their pockets.

During the winter, she boarded up her cabin and loaded a mule with a year's accumulation of her customers' dirty laundry and traveled to the distant hot springs in the Washoe Valley, where she scrubbed the clammy Washoe soil that the prospectors loudly cursed as that "damned blue stuff" out of their red shirts and black jeans, and mended them for the boys back home.

A spectacular serving of Eilley Orrum's famed pork and beans and batter biscuits was being dished up as Snowshoe Thompson arrived at her cabin. He unburdened himself of his pouch with a tremendous shrug, to the accompaniment of cheers from a scruffy group of Johntown citizens lounging on rugged wooden benches in front of a grand fire blazing in a stone fireplace large enough for a grizzly bear to stand in. The arrival of the mountain postman was an event susceptible to the analogy of a visit from Saint Nick. His pouch bulged with letters containing news from the infant towns of California and packages wrapped in burlap and twine with such luxuries as socks and eyeglasses. The Johntowners began whooping and clapping, the joyous squeals of little boys issuing from these gnarled, bearded men.

The creatures prancing around Snowshoe Thompson were an odd lot—prodigal, brawny, obstreperous, confabulating, a wise-cracking crew of shaggy, sagebrush-eating mortals. Among their number were those whom fate had lucklessly cast for key roles in the opening act of the epic comedy-tragedy soon to be played on the richest proscenium in the history of the world.

There was James Fennimore, a strapping, boozing former muleskinner who had killed a fellow in California and fled to the rough sanctuary of the Washoe, where he was known as "Old Virginny"—a monicker respectful of both the state of his origin and his menacing wish for anonymity.

When sober, which was not often, Old Virginny was considered to be the best placer miner in Gold Cañon. He marched unsteadily to work, balancing a rifle on one shoulder and a shovel on the other, somehow keeping one hand free to swig at a large brown bottle of a popular elixir of the Washoe—a raw distillation of potatoes said by some imbibers to be flavored with bat guano, dyed reddish brown by the addition of cinnabar, and known affectionately as tarantula juice.

Even more boisterous and equally as bibulous as Old Virginny was a stout, stealthy prospector whose face suggested a sagging balloon collared by limp chin whiskers. He was distinguished, if that word could ever apply to this creature of God, by one eye larger than the other—a pinkish eye that turned ruby red when he raised his voice, which was often. It was an eye that seemed to have overtaxed itself from excessive winking, an eye that perhaps had met with a keyhole accident, an eye through which

Henry Thomas Paige Comstock spied upon his surroundings warily, as if through a periscope.

The other miners called Comstock "Old Pancake," due to his unimaginative and miserly eating habits—pancakes in the morning, pancakes at noon, pancakes in the evening, with an occasional plate of Eilley Orrum's beans for variety. H. T. P. Comstock's public demeanor varied between bullying and bragging. As certain as he was that real treasure was hidden somewhere in the bleak Washoe, he feared he might not be the one to find it; he accordingly adopted the stratagem of spying on—and occasionally working with—every miner in Gold Cañon. When the great day came, he would be there, ready to claim his share, perhaps more than his share, of the inevitable Golconda. Comstock's braggart's sense of self-importance was to lead him to brand his name on the richest mining lode in history, and he was to die, fat and penniless, by his own hand, unable to live with the irony.

A wholly more cheery Johntowner was "Lucky Bill" Thorrington, who made his fortune in the California placers and returned to the Washoe to operate a public-spirited toll road and faro table at Devil's Gate. Lucky Bill was Nevada's first professional gambler. He was also its first humanitarian—he would give the winnings from his faro table to those who lost their roll, and his heart and pocketbook were open to any miner down on his luck. Bill Thorrington's propensity for helping any fellow in trouble was without discrimination, a fact that led to his regrettably early departure from this world, although his spirit endured in the reckless, good-natured fatalism of the men who toiled on Sun Mountain.

On his return hike across the Sierra, Snowshoe Thompson brought the Sacramento *Union* news of the singular demise of "Lucky Bill," who, having unwittingly provided shelter in his cabin one night to a fleeing horse thief, accepted with sunny equanimity the verdict of a roughshod jury of his peers that he should hang as an accessory. An inveterate gambler, Bill knew there was no reshuffling a stacked hand in a hostile house. "If they want to hang me, hang me. I'm no hog," he laughed—and he played the cards dealt him with high style, adjusting the noose around his own neck and singing at the top of his lungs the Washoe rendition of "The Last Rose of Summer," until the floor gave out from under him.

A gambler's ethic—more exactly, a gambler's stoicism—pervaded the mining camp. The prospectors knew Gold Cañon was nowhere but the bad side of purgatory. They seemed prepared to endure an eternity of searching for the secret of the Big Magnet while hoping for Lady Luck to take their hand and guide them to fortune—and she

THE HANGING OF LUCKY BILL THORRINGTON

that gives can take away, so if they lost a claim worth a fortune in the faro game of life, so be it.

Such a good-natured view of fate was shared by most of the miners washing down their pork and beans with tarantula juice at Eilley Orrum's—lads such as Sandy Bowers, a slow-thinking, optimistic muleskinner for whom Eilley had eyes, and Pete O'Reilly and Pat McLaughlin and Alvah Gould. It was just as well, for they were all to stumble about the edge of wealth, and most were to be snubbed by fate.

Two men in Gold Cañon did not subscribe to the blithe fatalism of their fellows. They were the Grosch brothers, Ethan Allen and Hosea Ballou, sons of a New York Universalist clergyman. Out to strike it rich in the West, the brothers drifted across the Sierras from the California placers in the early 1850s and by all recollection had been working the rills and crevices of Gold Cañon longer than anyone else. They lived alone, outside of the Johntown camp, in a bleak place called American Flats. They built a stone house of yellow rock and filled it with strange devices—bellows, a furnace, mortars, vials of chemicals, thick books—and spent each evening there alone, apart from the ribald company of their fellow prospectors. The rest of the boys considered them a bit touched in the head, an impression that was reinforced as the Grosches moved their prospecting gear beyond Devil's Gate, further than anyone else had ventured up the forbidding slopes of the mountain, where thin veins of the useless "blue stuff" oozed out of the coarse earth like coagulating blood from the wound of a giant desert beast.

The evening of Snowshoe Thompson's arrival was one of the rare occasions on which the Grosch brothers frequented Eilley Orrum's cabin. Even there they kept to themselves, eating alone on a far bench away from the warmth of the fire, not talking, and not drinking. The brothers were viewed with a suspicion that had festered into paranoia by H. T. P. Comstock. These strange birds knew something, of that he was sure. Witches, Comstock called them, a pair of he-witches who cooped themselves up at night with their vials and weird contraptions—trying to work up some curse over the mountain, to render it helpless, so they could find its secret!

Snowshoe Thompson had a package for the Grosches. Comstock's erubescent eye glowed like a fired coal as he twisted his neck to see what was inside. A book! Another damned thick book! What were prospectors, mountain men, doing with all those books? Old Pancake was no reading man, but he was strong on intuition; he knew that somewhere between those fancy leather covers was a key to the secret of the mountain. He vowed to find it out, if he had to follow those he-witches night and day.

The good beans and warm fire and tarantula juice were working their spell in the cabin. A miner started to fiddle an Irish jig and men began swinging each other around the floor, energetically trading off the two quite outnumbered women—buxom, corseted, laughing Eilley Orrum and plump, smiling, pretty Sarah Winnemucca, a Piute princess with a taste for firewater, the daughter of the great chief Winnemucca, a squaw for all seasons.

As the music began the Grosch brothers hurriedly packed up their new book and lurched out into the cold windy night. A "Washoe Zephyr" was blowing up—the local version of a tornado, a sudden mean windstorm that zipped down Sun Mountain with the whip and buck of a frenzied stallion, lifting scrub pine and firewood like matchsticks and blowing unfortunate mules called "Washoe Canaries" halfway down the canyon.

Comstock glanced anxiously about, assuring himself that the others were too wrapped up in the embrace of tarantula juice to take any notice, and followed the Grosch brothers out into the gathering storm.

Under the moonless sky the flickering light from the Grosches' stone house cast ghostly images on the damp Washoe earth. Comstock struggled against the contrary embrace of the wind and attached his person to the outer wall of the house the way a lizard clutches a tree trunk. He vowed to stick there all night through the storm—curse the storm!—until he learned the secret of the mysterious brothers Grosch.

Some people have a natural ability for foreign languages; Henry Comstock had one for stealth. His friends wagered that he would have weaseled his way out of his mother's womb were it not for the umbilical cord tying him in place. Comstock wished for such a natural anchor that howling night as the wind threatened to blow him away from his tiptoe perch below a window of the stone house. Around him the dust whirled in the crags of the mountain and the sagebrush crackled and snapped as if crushed by some giant unseen hand. But the determined spy held fast to his window, transfixed by the scene inside.

The most sophisticated of observers could not but have been startled at the image mirrored in Henry Comstock's looking-glass eye. The fantastic picture inside the mountain cabin suggested the work of a perversely imaginative painter attempting to transfer the legendary story of the Sorcerer's Apprentice to a frontier canvas.

Inside the cabin, giant leaping shadows were cast by an enormous fire of blazing sagebrush bales piled perilously high in a cavernous fireplace. The unnaturally bright light illuminated a roughhewn wooden workbench where the brothers huddled together as if for warmth in the blazing room; they were bent so close at their task that it was impossible to tell where Ethan Allen's beard ended and Hosea's beard began.

The shelves above the workbench were crammed with leather-backed volumes and vials and jars filled with liquids of amber and xanthous hues. The bench was cluttered with the ancient trappings of the alchemist's discipline—scales, test tubes, mortar bowl, and large bubble-bottomed retorts with long, pointed glass beaks that cast off shadows like anteaters.

Comstock watched Ethan Allen Grosch get up from the workbench and pump the canvas bellows of another fire kindled in a crude open oven on the cabin floor. "Damned Firebugs!" muttered the spy in the window as Ethan Allen built the fire in the crude furnace to a white heat. At the bench his brother beat and pounded in a mortar bowl the hated earth of the Washoe—the "blue stuff" that caked the miners' pores and clogged their mining rockers.

Hosea pounded the blue stuff into a fine powder, which Ethan Allen carefully placed inside the white hot furnace topped with strange glass tubing that ran to one of the beakers on the workbench. "Cooking dirt! The idiots are cooking dirt!" Comstock said to the coyote that was his only company on his icy perch, and he and the coyote had a good laugh.

It seemed as if an hour passed—indeed it was almost that—while the brothers watched the glass beaker with fierce attention. Finally Ethan Allen filled a test tube with nitric acid—Comstock tried to memorize the label on the thick brown bottle from which Grosch poured. Then Ethan Allen carefully removed a small dark button of metallic material from the bottom of the glass beaker. The faces of the brothers were

flushed and their eyes glittered as Allen held the vial of nitric acid up toward the fire and dropped the mysterious button into it with a trembling hand.

Slowly, it disappeared in the solution. The brothers did not speak but stared at one another in a religious fervor as if they themselves had re-created the miracle of water to wine. If Henry Comstock had known anything of what was in those books he so roundly cursed—if he had known a gram's worth about the sciences of metallurgy and chemistry—if indeed he could have read at all—he would have known that when the button of metal disappeared in the vial, it was the acid test for pure silver.

But Old Pancake knew none of this. Nor did he need to. In his demented mind greed instinctively fed cunning the way in a more balanced man knowledge might have contributed to wisdom. Comstock knew that, somehow, the brother-witches had discovered the secret of the mountain. He vowed to stay with them, closer than their shadows, until he discovered what it was—and found a way to take it from them.

The Grosch's discovery deserves to be recorded in vivid colors and with grand emotion. It was as dramatic and soaring as any scene from *The Arabian Nights*. It was more important in the history of the West than the driving of the Golden Spike. It should be painted and hung in the finest museum in the world as a portrayal of one of those rare moments in time when man stands at the threshold of new greatness and new madness simultaneously.

It would not be stretching the reaches of verisimilitude to suggest that in such a painting a genie would be coming out of the Grosches' little beaker—a featureless, button-shaped, silver blob—which would soon grow into a giant mountain of silver laced with gold. It would write new chapters in the history of the United States and scar the unblemished face of the West with industrialization. It would draw tens of thousands of natural gamblers—people who were willing to speculate with their own lives—to the foreboding mountain upon whose dusty skirts would grow for a moment in time the richest city in the world—and it would twist the fates of men and women with the caprice of a cat playing with a ball of yarn.

The first to suffer the dark fortune of the mountain were the Grosches. But the mountain did not take its vengeance swiftly; that would be too easy on the pair who had dared discover its secret. It instead let the Grosches feverishly follow the mirage of wealth, like two men lost in the desert racing toward a shimmering lake always just a few yards away.

That Kismet night the fateful button of silver dissolved in the vial the brothers spent before the dying fire in low conversation that was not what one would altogether expect from the sons of a minister. It would seem that a spore of the dementia of Henry Comstock's predatory brain had blown from his window ledge into the ears of the two men and lodged in that part of the brain which medical science tells us enables the human animal to make reasoned judgments. For by the time the Washoe dawn broke reluctantly gray and the faint hint of daylight shone dully on the glass beakers and·tubings of their alchemists' equipment, the Grosch brothers had decided to horde the precious secret of the blue black stuff and to divine a way to take the riches of the entire mountain all by themselves.

It was in pursuit of this unsound proposition that the Grosch brothers set out the next morning with Old Pancake, blue from his vigil but red with determination, puffing behind them. The daily routine of the Grosch brothers did not vary for the next several months, and neither did that of their shadow. They prospected their way up Gold Cañon looking for a spot where the blue black mud would ooze like syrup and the blue was as bright as a fine spring night's sky. They knew from their books that this would be the spot near the heart of the mountain. The Grosches found such a place above a particularly unattractive outcropping that they marked on their penciled maps as the "Divide," where Gold Cañon leveled off its ascent below the crown of Sun Mountain. Here the blue black goo pulsed in great veins under the earth and glistened with specks of gold as it disappeared down into the very heart of the Big Magnet.

A historical digression is in order here since the Grosch brothers have been as ill treated by history as they were by life. The scriveners of Western America have by and large taken as gospel the speculations of that unique breed of scholars known as mining historians who have labeled mere blunderers as the real discoverers of the Comstock Lode and denied the Grosches the honor. Pages deeper and harder to read than these have been filled arguing this subject, an exercise that seems to the present authors to violate both human decency and common sense. The efforts of the experts to keep the lean and bearded visages of the Brothers Grosch off a Comstock commemorative stamp, should such a gem of the philatelic art come down the pike, appear the more myopic since many of the same authorities who question whether the Grosches actually penetrated the Comstock Lode proper tell us that despite the unreal riches taken from the Washoe earth, some 90 percent of the lode remains hidden in the mountain. The problem is that no one knows just where. A fair-minded nonexpert might observe that since the high sultans of mining lore are reduced to divining-rod status as to the whereabouts of most of the Comstock Lode, they are not your best witness as to whether the two Grosches did or did not dig into some part of it. The Grosches of course did; they unearthed the secret of the mountain's silver at a time when the stuff was almost literally oozing out of the mountain and all other prospectors were throwing the riches away. The reader pursuing a further interest in this topic should be warned that some historians will propose that two Irishmen, Pete O'Reilly

MINERS THREW AWAY THE ACCURSED "BLUE STUFF"

and Pat McLaughlin, made the formal discovery of the Comstock treasure, as if anything was done formally in those days. Yet the two Irishmen had no more clue that they were digging into silver than if they were digging into peanut butter. History thus written will not dissolve in the cold water of common sense.

But history was meaner to the Grosches than even the historians were. Not riches nor even fame but cruel and unusual fates awaited them.

As the sons of the minister stood bowed in the wind on the slope of Sun Mountain staring at the vein of blue black stuff as if at the jugular of life itself, they knew they were the first mortals to learn the mountain's secret—that the blue black mud the miners tossed away as they picked and scratched for gold was actually infinitely more valuable silver ore—a double treasure as it were, because the blue black stuff also contained a generous helping of gold that could be extracted along with the silver when one knew how, as the Grosch brothers did. They also knew that it would take far more than the gold-dust pans and rockers of placer miners to extract the treasure from its hiding place deep inside the mountain.

"Para trabajar un amina de plata se necesita una mina de oro" is a Spanish miners' proverb that loosely translates, "It takes a gold mine to develop a silver mine," which is to say it costs a lot of money. Men would have to burrow into the earth like moles to trace the vein of silver on its subcutaneous course. That, of course, required costly equipment, and the Grosch brothers divided their year according to the dictates of this reality. In the fall they crossed the Sierra to California, where they spent the winter months attempting to find money enough to pay for the mules, winches, and laborers necessary to mine their claim when the snow melted in the spring and the rich Washoe earth was once again vulnerable to nature's pickpockets.

The secret of the mountain became the compulsion of the Grosches. Had their sense of conspiracy been a few degrees less feverish, they might have found adequate partners to share in the expense and excitement of tracking the monster vein. But their need for assistance was overcome by their fanaticism about secrecy. They returned to the Washoe with but one worker, a strapping young Canadian named Richard Bucke, from whom they kept their true plans, and the same sad mule with which they had left.

The brothers and their wage slave set to work on the surface of the vein, attempting to accomplish with back muscle and sweat what winch and derrick should do. Their first assays proved the ore was richer than they had dared dream, and Ethan Allen wrote his minister-father a worldly letter, brazenly speculating on the riches to come and describing the beloved rich earth. In a letter dated November 22, 1856, Allen and Hosea had written: "We found two veins of silver at the forks of Gold Cañon . . . One of these veins is a perfect monster." And again on the eighth of June 1857: "The rock of the vein looks beautiful, is very soft, and will work remarkably easy. The show of metallic silver produced by exploding it in damp gunpowder is very promising. The rock is iron, and its colors are violet-blue, blue-black and greenish-black."

The Grosch brothers had hopes of rigging heavy machinery and beginning to mine their claim in earnest. These high expectations rested on the one potential investor they felt they could trust with their secret, George Brown, a kindly old man, a California stationmaster. After their first assay they had written Brown urgently requesting his financial assistance. He had replied that he would sell out his business and come with his life savings of $600. It would be more than sufficient for food and machinery and labor through the fall.

They ventured to Eilley Orrum's cabin for a celebratory dinner of bacon and stewed rabbit, the luster of the occasion dimmed only by the fact that they could not tell anyone what they were celebrating. An uncharacteristically vocal Hosea delivered to Eilley Orrum a lecture on the quality of Washoe rocks, and when he was done she was blushing with the full fruit of knowledge of the important things distinguishing quartzite and hornblende and limestone. As his brother cautioned him to silence, Hosea told Eilley in guarded terms of their claim and said that they would be rich and she, too, would be rich. But he did not say how. He did not mention the blue stuff.

The time for Brown's arrival came and passed. The brothers grew desperate. It was already August. In a few months the canyon would wear the white coat of winter and there could be no more work until the next year. By then others might discover the secret. They couldn't delay, so they resorted to the unrewarding work of panning gold to get money to continue their claim.

Trying to do two jobs at once, Hosea one day got careless. His rusty pick slipped and stabbed through his boot into the skin in the hollow of his foot. He bathed the offended limb and pulled his worn black boot on. He limped a little, but he did not stop working. The brothers were racing the great hourglass of the seasons. It became a race to the death.

The Grosches' eating habits in the months since the rabbit and bacon feast at Eilley Orrum's had grown lamentably more in line with Old Pancake's three squares a day of baker's dough. The brothers were saving money on food so they could pay the wages of the Canadian, who worked like a winch hoist. The undernourished Hosea was no match for the fever that cooked his body and the poisonous red line that crept up his leg. Desperately Ethan Allen enlisted the aid of the ever-present Comstock to bathe his brother's foot with hot compresses while he worked the gold rockers for the money to keep the claim going. Comstock took the occasion of his act of Christian charity to interrogate Hosea in his delirium about the secret.

The ministrations of this double-angel of mercy seemed to have some effect. Hosea's

Overleaf:
SIERRA BLIZZARD

fever lessened and the swelling in his foot receded. He said he felt well enough to get up out of his bunk. His neck was stiff and he had trouble swallowing and chewing, but otherwise he declared himself fit as a fiddle. The brothers rejoiced that night. Soon George Brown must arrive and the pain of the secret would be but a dull memory.

But word came the next morning that their messiah had been murdered. George Brown had been shot in the back by desperadoes on his way to the Washoe. The $600 was gone. At that ghastly news Hosea's mouth stretched taut over his teeth in a terrifying grimace. He never changed his expression. Chills shook his body like a butter churn and his eyebrows were frozen in a bas-relief of surprise. Ethan Allen could not feed his brother or pour a drink between his tight, grinning lips. His jaws were a vice, and the most pitiful of sounds came from his throat in the place of words. An awesome fear in his eyes betrayed the mask of mirth that had become his face. He died smiling. It was September 2, 1857. The Grosch brothers had known the secret for two years.

Hosea Grosch was dressed up splendidly to meet his maker. His brother insisted there would be no red flannel shirt and black jeans that were the mufti of the Washoe miners. Ethan Allen instead bought his brother a new suit and a white collar and insisted to a Washoe dry goods merchant who tried to sell him just the front of a shirt that his brother would be buried with a shirt on his back too. The sartorially elegant Hosea was lowered into the earth of Gold Cañon in a proper pine box while the citizens of Johntown stood by in silent salute and the Chinese workers known thereabouts as the "Celestials" plunked at homemade stringed instruments. Ethan Allen and the brawny Canadian lifted the largest boulders they could handle atop Hosea's grave to cheat the coyotes of their picnic. It was the finest funeral Johntown had ever seen. It took every cent Ethan Allen had in his pocket and left him $60 in debt, but that seemed a small matter compared to the proper repose of his beloved brother. It would prove a fateful matter for him.

Ethan Allen worked at the Gold Cañon placers washing gravel for gold until he had made the $60 to pay for Hosea's last rites. He wrote his father a lengthy letter filled with lamentations buffered by Puritan resignation at the loss of his fraternal partner. He could take solace only in the fact that the secret for which Hosea had died was still safe; he pledged to carry on alone to bring the family dream of riches to fruition. It was late in the fall when Ethan Allen paid off the last dollar of the funeral expenses and made ready to cross the mountains for California to secure new backing. The thin crust of winter was in the air, and the first blizzards of the season had already dusted the High Sierra. The other Johntowners warned him against undertaking such a journey. But for Ethan Allen to sit out the winter in repose by his brother's fresh grave would be to mock the effort that had occasioned his death. He must go. Bucke, the Canadian, who no longer drew a salary and still had no inkling of the secret, was itching to get back to California and volunteered to brave the crossing with the remaining Grosch brother.

In his rush to leave the Washoe, Ethan Allen enlisted the aid of Old Pancake, who had continued to spy on one Grosch brother without any appreciable diminishment of the energy he had expended spying on two. Ethan Allen wanted his house guarded, and since Comstock was always lurking about, he seemed a logical man for the task. Comstock's red eye blinked nervously as he weighed the proposition put to him: he was to stay in the stone cabin that winter and guard the assay apparatus and a black wooden box that Ethan Allen had nailed tight with papers, books, ore samples, and coded diagrams of his claims inside. For such service Comstock would receive one fourth of the claims that Ethan Allen would develop when he returned with new backing the next spring. Old Pancake warily agreed, making Ethan Allen put their "contract" in writing. He was sure he couldn't lose. If the last Grosch returned, he would have one-fourth with no labor; if he did not, the secret was in the black box, and he would have it all.

The afternoon was deceptively clear and warm as the Canadian and Ethan Allen Grosch began the steep ascent up the Sierra trail. The donkey was piled high with saddlebags of food, warm clothing, rifles, and ammunition—the indispensable items of winter survival. But there was one valuable Ethan Allen did not trust to any repository save his own breast. He clutched a heavy package in a waterproof bag inside his shirt. It was the secret—ore samples, maps, charts, and claims to the treasure of the Big Magnet.

The slow-moving trio reached the 9000-foot eastern summit of the Sierra before the fury of the winter fell upon them. The first storm was followed piggyback by a second and then a third in seemingly endless succession, until the blizzards obscured the vast frozen basin that held Lake Tahoe 3000 feet below. The Truckee trail was now lost in snow, but the two staggered forward down the slope, attempting with freezing hands to part the curtain of snow before them. When at last they reached Squaw Valley their food had gone and the donkey was bent and creased like a child's plaything and whimpering miserably. It turned its sad wet eyes away from the pine scrubs that Ethan Allen gently offered it as the only edibles they had. Ethan Allen was sobbing, and his tears turned instantly to ice and were snapped off his face by the gale-force winds. He slowly unpacked the faithful animal. Closing his eyes in grief, he placed the cold muzzle of his gun into the warm furry ear of the poor braying thing and he put the beast of burden to rest.

The Canadian, who was more the stranger to the beast, stripped her to the bone and roasted her meat. They carried what they could of it with them in backpacks, leaving all else behind in the storm save their firearms. Through serial blizzards they attempted to cross the floor of Squaw Valley on snowshoes hand-fashioned from green saplings. During this entire blinding white ordeal Ethan Allen clutched to his chest the package that was more precious to him than his soul. His gloved hands had become so numb that he could no longer feel what he was holding and he had to crane his stiff neck downward to see if the tiny treasure was still riding in the kangaroo pouch of his bosom.

That night the two men dug into the snow for warmth and awoke to the hot foul breath of wolves sniffing at their feet. During the next two days they reached the western ridge of Squaw Valley. They consumed the last of the donkey in ritual communion. Flash rains and wet rolling waves of sleet drowned their guns and they would no longer fire. Their drenched clothes became frozen like armor, and they had to beat their arms and legs against tree trunks to break the ice so they could move.

Ethan Allen realized he could no longer protect his treasure from the elements. He feared the ink on his maps would run and become unreadable, which would be as bad as losing them entirely. He took the package from under his crusted jacket and carefully secured it in a fallen tree trunk that was dry from the elements, covering it with twigs and small rocks and rolling a boulder in front of the hollow of the tree. He cut a cross in the fallen trunk and burned the location into his memory. He told the Canadian not to look.

The two men crashed and rolled down the snow-banked hills from Squaw Valley, often crawling on all fours like animals, taking the fury of the continuing blizzard on their backs. As the weather slackened slightly to a duller roar they collapsed. The sleep of the exhausted or the dead in these circumstances of inhuman ordeal can be much the same, and when a party of miners came across them and lifted them tenderly onto dog sleds the rescuers were not sure whether the pair were dead or alive.

Bucke lived to return to Canada, minus one leg and part of a foot that the blizzard claimed as souvenirs. Ethan Allen was delirious for weeks, and on December 19, 1857, he sat up, looked around curiously, and died.

He had never said a word to his wilderness companion about his secret. It wasn't until years later that the Canadian learned he had hid something valuable in the tree trunk. He didn't have a clue where it was.

This would be a good place to stop and take our bearings on the mountain. For geography, and geology, will play the kind of roles in this story usually reserved for the deus ex machina of Greek tragedies or the villainous landlord of nineteenth-century farce. The accidents of geography and geology that created the Big Magnet were to reign imperiously over all those who were drawn to it. In the beginning, it was a dismal

THE BEAST OF BURDEN IS PUT TO REST

prospect. Even the stout Cortés, had he stood on some high peak looking down on the Washoe Mountains, might have paled at the prospect of exploring such unrewarding terrain. There was no hint of treasure or signal of grandeur. The vista of the Big Magnet was that of the bottom of God's own spittoon, and a dry bottom at that. So it was with all Nevada. Nevada has the arguable distinction of being the sole state of the Union that is wholly contained—if one disallows the tiny green patch of the spendid Sierra Nevada that occupies a picture-postcard-sized square on Nevada's western border—in that singular portion of the North American continent known as the Great Basin.

From a bird's-eye view, the Great Basin is a huge triangular-shaped brownout approximating 200,000 square miles and stretching from the east slope of the Sierra Nevada to the west slope of the mighty Rocky Mountain range, which rises like some giant brontosaur's backbone dividing the western third of the United States from the sandbox of the prairie states and the finery of the East. The Basin was so named by Colonel J. C. Frémont, the frontier explorer, who displayed, if not a poet's soul, a plumber's wisdom, because it does indeed resemble a vast sink on which the plug has been pulled. The floor of the Great Basin is what the Great Lakes might look like if they too dried up. The washboard terrain of the Great Basin is ridged with minor north-south mountain ranges running parallel to the grander Rockies and the Sierra, and divided with arid valleys spotted with sagebrush and alkali sinks that broaden occasionally into deserts. Timber grows only at high altitudes, and agriculture more ambitious than a beanstalk requires extensive irrigation. There is little rain, and there are more dry riverbeds than rivers. What few there are have no outlet to the sea; they flow aimlessly and eventually sink into the ground.

Dan De Quille, the nom de plume used by William Wright, the distinguished and knowledgeable mining editor of the Virginia City *Territorial Enterprise*, once explained the laughable condition of the rivers of Nevada in the words of an old mountaineer and prospector:

> The way it came about was in this wise: The Almighty, at the time he was creatin' and fashionin' of this here yearth, got along to this section late on Saturday evening. He had finished all of the Great Lakes, like Superior, Michigan, Huron, Erie, and them—had made the Ohio, Missouri, And Mississippi rivers, and, as a sort of wind-up, was about to make a river that would be far ahead of anything he had yet done in that line. So he started in and traced out Humboldt River, and Truckee River, and Walker River, and Reese River, and all the other rivers, and he was leadin' of them along, calkerlatin' to bring 'em all together into one big boss river and then lead that off and let it empty into the Gulf of Mexico or the Gulf of California, as that might be most convenient; but as he was bringin' down and leadin' along the several branches—the Truckee, Hum-

boldt, Carson, Walker, and them—it came on dark and instead of trying to carry out the original plan, he jist tucked the lower ends of the several streams into the ground, whar they have remained from that day to this.

As the Great Basin mountain ranges are poor brothers to the Sierras and the Rockies, so its rivers are poor sisters to the other great western rivers whose drainage basins rim the Great Basin top and bottom—the wild Columbia connecting the northwest to the Pacific Ocean, the feisty Colorado to the Gulf of California, the expansive Rio Grande to the Gulf of Mexico. The broad part of the Great Basin triangle includes the lower portions of Oregon and Idaho, and as the triangle narrows to an apex pointing into the heart of the southwest the Basin takes in both the sandy western half of Utah and Death Valley in California. But the lion's share of this forlorn triangle is taken up by another inverted triangle. This is Nevada.

It will be apparent by now to the reader that Nevada is not God's Green Acre, and indeed to this day the leading citizens of the Sagebrush State have been at a loss to find any productive use for the large sections of its sprawling dusty landscape other than the testing of atomic bombs. The early Spaniards despaired of exploring this steep barren expanse, and, as we have seen, the westward movement brushed by Nevada as a necessary ugliness on the way to California. Were a hungry giant to eat the states, Georgia would taste of peaches, Vermont of syrup, Florida of grapefruit, and Nevada of monosodium glutamate. Yet beneath the scruffy face of Nevada waited a fortune that would put shame to the tinsel legend of King Solomon's Mines.

A miner's bedtime story of the great silver mine in the sky was told in the Washoe as the creosote brush flared in the campfire and the animals of the night made impolite noises somewhere out in the surrounding darkness. It was a high tale of a glorious mine known only to the red man and of a miner who had saved an Indian chief's life and in payment was brought to the mine blindfolded so he could not find his way back by himself. A large flat rock was rolled back from the mouth of a cavern, and when his eye bandanna was removed the miner was nearly blinded by the brilliant effulgence of the pure silver within. His Indian guide handed him a tomahawk and indicated he could carve out a piece. The miner chopped carefully at the bright silver roof of the cave and loosened a shining lump of pure silver the size of a saddle. But the Indian came and took the tomahawk away even as the silver was hanging by a single thread. His time in the cave was up, and the miner had to leave without his treasure. The moral of the story was that you had to be quick to get silver. As practical lore it was as useful as the tall tales the prospectors valued as facts of history—tales of the well-known treasures of Potosí and Montezuma, of the Incas and the Aztecs who drank from silver goblets and ate with silver spoons and danced by the light of the silvery moon. The Washoe prospectors particularly enjoyed the story of the Indian who found the world-famous silver mine at Potosí, Peru, in 1545 by chasing a goat up a mountain. When the naked native grabbed a bush to keep his balance, it came out by the roots and there underneath was a mound of glittering silver. Once you found a silver vein, the riches were as easy to reach as taking the top off a jar of marmalade went the miners' legend. The legend did the boys of the Washoe a disservice. The miners' fervent beliefs about the ready availability of silver once you located it were to prove sorrowfully wrong.

The mountain had the deck stacked from the start. For the muckers, as miners of silver bonanza were called, the immutable laws of geology were a cold departure from the warm frontier legend of that great silver mine in the sky. In the California Gold Rush, every man with the price of a pan could have a chance at finding the precious stuff and a good many did; placer miners for the most part rarely had to dig far below the surface. In Nevada, deep silver mining became Big Business, where the money—with a helping of luck—made the difference between winners and losers. The rigors of Washoe geography, which served so well for so long to conceal the mountain's treasure, made it as difficult and costly as possible to dig it out of the earth and separate it from other minerals. The treasure of the Big Magnet was fabulous in its excess but equally stunning in the sudden way the mountain would perniciously snatch back its sacrament from the cupped chalice of one mucker's calloused hands and proceed to shamelessly tempt another. Thus, those two obstinate elements of nature—geography and geology—became the deus ex machina that would alternately make the epic of Virginia City both high tragedy and black comedy.

Part Two

OYSTERS
IN THE
DESERT

H. T. P. Comstock shivered through the winter in the Grosch brothers' yellow stone house in American Flats. His first thought upon waking and his last before going to sleep was of the mysterious he-witches' box. In his fitful slumber his numbed brain was filled with a recurring dream of a golden mountain—its surface bursting with nuggets, its rich bulging sides held together by the force of silver rays of light. Evenings, after his pauper's repast, he hallucinated a fantastic banquet where he presided over a mixed grill of jewel-encrusted pheasant and solid-gold pancakes and the champagne flowed like melting snow down the Sierra slopes. His winter of Midas-dreams ended in hysterics when Snowshoe Thompson brought the bad news of Ethan Allen Grosch's arctic death.

Comstock tore open the box in a rage fit for a mad bull. He ripped apart the maps and books and smashed the retorts and crucibles with the zeal of a person pounding a stake into a vampire's heart. He then put the torch to the laboratory. As he watched the combustible remains curl slowly in the flames, Old Pancake clumsily stuffed the pockets of his tattered outcoat with a few crumbling specimens of the blue stuff; souvenirs of witches! Mumbling a final goddamn, Comstock mounted his unfortunate one-eyed mustang, a creature so swaybacked that its master's legs hit the ground from the saddle, and stumbled up the canyon to claim his destiny.

Old Pancake carried his "contract" from Ethan Allen Grosch close to his vest. He was convinced this paper gave him the legal right to be King of the Mountain; the witches were dead, long live the King! All its treasures were in his dominion. Comstock rode into Johntown a changed man. He almost glowed with a sense of new-found self-importance. It was as if he had gone from rags to riches without changing his rags. He sought out two Piute braves with time on their hands and hired them to wash gravel for him. The two braves took to following their benefactor everywhere. Old Pancake explained to his puzzled fellow Johntowners that his strange entourage was necessary because he was an important figure now, too busy to wash his gold, or his hands, for himself.

Old Virginny Fennimore mused on Comstock's sudden exuberance. It was just possible that Old Pancake had stumbled onto the so-called secret of the Grosches—a "Lost Ledge" the boys talked about half in jest, half seriously. And if he hadn't found it, he might have an idea where to look. Fennimore followed Comstock into little-explored rills and crevices on the other side of Sun Mountain.

But Comstock's wanderings defied sense. He seemed to spend hours just contemplating the mountain. Yet, despite the chorus of jeers from the Gold Cañon prospectors at Old Pancake's comings and goings on his pathetic one-eyed mustang, the man had a certain absurd dignity. He was apart from the other Johntowners: a throneless king in exile with his two Piute equerries, regally ignoring the mindless mockery of the mob.

Old Virginny grew tired of chasing Comstock around the mountain. A seasoned hunter, he decided his quarry wasn't worth the catch. The man was wandering in circles. Fennimore reached this laborious conclusion high up on the north slope of Sun Mountain. Comstock had just gone round a bend; Old Virginny let him go. He took an unhealthy swig of tarantula juice from the bottle in his pack and had just begun the two-mile trek back to Gold Cañon when a tawny yellow outcropping on the slope caught his miner's eye. So the trip wouldn't be for nothing, he staked a claim by placing a wrinkled piece of paper under a flat quartz rock. On the paper was written, "James Fennimore, February 22, 1858."

Back in Johntown the boys were celebrating Washington's birthday with holiday cups of tarantula juice. They toasted Fennimore's claim as if General George himself had staked it out. It was "Old Virginny's Ledge"—and it was agreed by one and all, amid uproarious laughter, that no one else could ever prospect that claim, up there with the crows on the mountainside. Old Virginny went back to his normal full-time occupation of drinking distilled spirits and never bothered to dig in his ledge. In a few years, the paper under the rock would be the most valuable parchment on the mountain.

Comstock swelled with dementia. That the Grosches had confused him with their evil scribblings was a bitter pill—but Old Virginny's claim on his home turf was an outright act of aggression. Old Pancake counterattacked. Early the next morning he began the meticulous process of placing paper "claims" on every likely wart and blemish of the earth. He kept stuffing his grimy, pencil-marked "locations" under rocks and pinning them to trees until the upper slope of Gold Cañon was a virtual patchwork quilt of his claims. Then, to protect his newly conquered empire, he took up daily sentry duty in front of the twin pilasters at Devil's Gate. As groups of bearded Johntowners shuffled up the canyon, he challenged them each: Halt! All who passed were thus alerted to his divine sovereignty over this domain—this was "Comstock's Lode." And so it came forever to be called.

The lode to which Comstock pinned his name is a giant vein of silver-bearing decomposed quartz extending nearly five miles north-to-south across the eastern slopes of Sun Mountain. It ran as much as 3000 feet long below the earth and at least 2500 feet deep—no one knows to this day just how far down it goes. The elusive ledges of silver ore that constituted only a fraction of the lode—geologists' estimates make it as minuscule as 1/500th—darted downward, upward, and sideways with all the sense of the direction of fireflies, occasionally breaking through to the surface amid piles of decomposed rock miners call outcroppings. These silver capillaries lay partially exposed at the mouths of twin canyons running down the eastern face of the mountain. At the rim of Gold Cañon, which runs southeasterly, a flat area called the "Divide" separates Gold Cañon from Six Mile Cañon, which begins somewhat lower on the northeastern side of the slope and runs down to the Carson River. "Gold" was finally discovered atop both canyons by Old Virginny, Old Pancake, and their luckless friends, only it wasn't gold—it was far richer silver sulfide bearing gold in a proportion of about one-third gold to two thirds of the more valuable silver ore, the familiar blue black stuff the prospectors were throwing away.

Times were tough in Gold Cañon by the winter of 1858 and many of the boys were ordering Eilley Orrum's beans and telling her to hold the pork. The little gold that was left to find in the lower canyon was so flaky that the Washoe prospectors took to mixing it with "real" California gold dust to make it respectable before bagging it to sell in Placerville. After New Year's, as if by resolution, they began moving up the canyon toward the Divide in search of something more substantial. This did nothing to quiet Comstock's territorial trembles.

On a cold, gray January day, Comstock's worst fears were realized. He heard screams and hoots and whoops of joy—among them those of his mortal enemy Old Virginny—coming from a rise up near the Divide. Sensing that Old Virginny had come upon the Lost Ledge of the Grosches, Comstock prowled through the underbrush to a small precipice looking down Crown Point Ravine, where he spied four aggressors— Old Virginny, "Big French John," Aleck Henderson, and Jack Yount—howling over a shimmering pan of gold just exhumed and washed from a red clay eruption in the Washoe snow.

Comstock crashed down the snow-banked hill, making noises about claim jumping loud enough to start an avalanche. But the bibulous Old Virginny and his jubilant friends would take none of Comstock's lip; they replied that he could claim he made every tree and that still wouldn't make him God. They busied themselves washing the gold out of the Washoe dirt while Old Pancake sputtered like an unattended teakettle. The quartet had uncovered the southern outcroppings of the Comstock Lode and the hill they were standing on was soon to earn the lasting nickname of Gold Hill, the site of famous mines such as the Yellow Jacket and the Crown Point.

By spring the entire Johntown mining camp had moved up the canyon to Gold Hill.

Eilley Orrum seduced some Washoe teamsters into hauling her log cabin there. The transplanted prospectors spread out over the Divide looking for gold, and on June 8, 1859, two easygoing boys from the Emerald Isle, Pete O'Reilly and Pat McLaughlin, found it. They were digging a spring near the head of Six Mile Cañon for water to wash their ore when they chanced to rinse some of the curiously yellow sand in their rockers. The bottom was covered with pure sparkling gold dust. This event is enshrined in most conventional history books as the "official" discovery of the Comstock Lode. O'Reilly and McLaughlin were smiling leprechaun smiles when Comstock rode up on his sad horse in his usual uninvited fashion. Old Pancake's alarm-eye glowed red at the sight of the gold, but this time he had a different story to tell. He congratulated the Irishmen on their find. The gold was theirs all right, no question about that. Only there was the small matter that he, H. T. P. Comstock, owned their water, and the rights to develop the land as well. Why, hadn't he and Manny Penrod and Old Virginny bought the water rights above Six Mile Cañon from what-was-his-first-name Caldwell just last year, and some old sluice boxes and the 160 acres that went with it? Comstock said he'd wait there and watch their gold while they checked with anyone, if they needed to check such common knowledge.

O'Reilly and McLaughlin had the look of canaries about to be eaten by a cat. As any placer miner could tell you, you can't mine gold without water—lots of water. Comstock smiled at them like a bubbling spring. There was a simple way out of this: the Irish could trade a portion of their claim—say one hundred feet, as they would have much more than that—in exchange for Comstock's water rights. All they'd have to do was sign a paper to make it legal.

The boys agreed right on the spot. Their strike became the world-famous Ophir Mine, the first Bonanza on the lode. Comstock had of course never recorded his at best disputable claim to the water rights, as he never bothered to post any of his overreaching claims other than by the not inconsiderable public conveyance of his own loud mouth. Comstock got his silver and gold on the strength of his brass.

When the deed was done Comstock raced off as fast as his broken-down horse would carry him to Old Virginny's Gold Hill hovel. He would cut Manny Penrod in on the deal, but he had different plans for Old Virginny, who had started this damnable business of other people staking claims on Comstock's mountain. Old Virginny used to say that every night he had a contest between "my appetite and my drinketite." This was one of the nights when his drinketite won. He was so deep in wine that he was actually happy to see Comstock. The two prospectors drank long into the evening, and

when Old Pancake walked away he had swapped his half-blind horse and a bottle of Sazerac for Old Virginny's share of the Six Mile Cañon site. It was not until Old Virginny sobered up the next day that he realized his new horse was in need of a Seeing Eye dog. In a short time those few feet in the Ophir were worth $60,000, prompting Old Virginny to complain in the happy losers' spirit of the Comstock about having a $60,000 horse but not being able to afford a saddle to ride him.

Ushering in summer, the torrid Washoe Zephyrs huffed about the unprotected mountain slopes and knocked some of the boys off their feet as they continued to scratch into the gritty skin of the Comstock Lode outcroppings. As word reached the California placers, miners shouldered their pickaxes and took the six-day hike over the Sierra. The Gold Hill settlement sprawled over the Divide and a new tent city rose uncertainly on the steep side of Sun Mountain above Six Mile Cañon. The first business was a bar consisting of a canvas shade over a plank spread between two barrels. But claims proliferated like measle spots over the face of the mountain and soon there were ten bars and a hundred tents and hundreds of "coyote holes" where miners without the price of a roof burrowed into the side of the mountain for warmth at night and pulled up a clump of sagebrush for a pillow.

Prospectors and whores with little else to do played cards on the flimsy wooden floors of canvas shacks and booze seemed to spill from every orifice of the sweating, stinking city which as yet had no name. Then one night while walking home under a summer full moon, Old Virginny, who had not suffered the debilitating effects of sobriety during this period, stumbled and dropped the last bottle of his stash on the rocky crust of the mountainside. He fell to his knees and swilled the last drops of tarantula juice from the remaining cup-shaped bottom of the bottle. Staying put on his knees, he made of the horrifying incident a baptismal party by shouting to the sky, "I christen this place Virginia Town." Thus in 1859 Virginia City was born under a drunken moon, and swaddled in the kerosene glow of wobbly tents.

At the Ophir diggings, O'Reilly and McLaughlin, with their partners of Comstock & Company, were washing $50 to $75 a day from a single tub of crushed ore and some of the Gold Hill digs were doing almost as well. While this was a munificent sum compared to the bare five dollars the boys used to eke out on a good day in Gold Cañon, it was therefore all the more cause for alarm when the surface of the loose outcroppings was picked bare and the prospectors were forced to dig deeper into the ground with pickaxes and shovels. This slowed the process, and also the profits, as the ore now had to be crushed before washing and the ledges often dove deep into the ground.

Piles of discarded ore, which miners call "tailings," began to rise near the diggings, and Comstock led his fellow toilers in a chant of overheated cursing that shook the tent-saloons after the day's work was done. Always it was the "goddamned blue mud" that clogged their rockers and prevented them from turning their dreams to gold. This saloon grumbling grew louder through the chill summer evenings, and Virginia City was not a happy place to be.

During the last week of June 1859, a man named J. F. Stone rode up from the Truckee River Crossing to look things over. Stone ambled up Gold Cañon past the bent backs of hundreds of miners until he happened upon the Ophir Mine and a mound of tailings resembling a blue black dunghill. Perhaps it was little more than a visitor's curiosity that made the Truckee Meadows rancher get off his horse and climb this god-forsaken trash heap, but it was a prospector's eye that guided his rough hands over the scorned rock discarded by the placer miners. Following his instinct, Stone methodically selected samples of the ore, placed them in his saddlebags, and rode back.

When he descended the California slope of the mountains, Stone asked his friend B. A. Harrison, a rancher who lived near Grass Valley, to examine the strange rocks from the other side. Harrison, finding a substance he had not known, passed the crumbling rock to Judge James Walsh, a respected jurist and also the best judge of minerals in El Dorado County. But he, too, found it totally alien to his eye.

It remained for Melville Atwood, the celebrated frontier assayer and chemist, to perform the crucial test in the fires of his crucible in Grass Valley. Atwood made assay after assay, until his face flushed red in the heat of the great kiln. After twelve hours, he shook his head in disbelief at his findings. Never was there ore like this. The strange blue stuff was almost solid silver: Four thousand seven hundred and ninety-one dollars to the ton, two-thirds in silver, the rest an ore-soft mass of gold. The lost secret of the Grosch brothers was being thrown away into the Zephyr winds by the founding fools of Washoe.

Late that night, Atwood summoned the judge to the back door of his office. Judge Walsh, true to the tradition of competitive free enterprise, immediately swore the assay-ist to secrecy by promising him two hundred feet in the new bonanza. The judge shucked his robes, packed hurriedly, and rode out with a partner into the Sierra night, their saddlebags brimming with gold to buy up control of the Comstock Lode.

The judge's secret lasted less than twenty-four hours. Atwood, also true to the tradition of competitive free enterprise, squealed. When the judge looked back from atop the Sierras the next day, he spied half of Grass Valley starting up the trail behind him. Atwood's excited reports of a great silver discovery hit San Francisco and the communities around the Bay like a flash flood from the swollen northern rivers; the traditional lure of California gold was replaced by the new magnet of Nevada silver.

Judge Walsh and his sidekick, Joe Woodworth, made their way up Gold Cañon to Virginia City to negotiate for the Ophir; they got there not a moment too soon; the founding fools were unloading their claims for a song. The placer miners who were accustomed to dealing with surface ore had no patience with chasing it down into the earth. Comstock had already sold a sixth interest in his part of the claim to a Mexican named Maldonado for a pair of mules, a transaction that would eventually make the asses worth $3 million each. McLaughlin pocketed $2500 in cash from George Hearst, a city slicker who had hurried over from San Francisco a few days after Walsh and managed to beat the Grass Valley jurist to the punch. Hearst became the first official millionaire among the Comstock nabobs and bought his son, William Randolph, a newspaper as a present. Comstock, suspicious of such sudden interest, was not so hasty but after summer-long negotiations sold out his remaining claims to Judge Walsh for $11,000, cash-on-the-barrelhead. Hearst and Walsh eventually joined forces to wrest control of the Ophir from its original owners, who walked around Virginia City boasting that they had fleeced "those crazy Californians."

It was the beginning of two glorious decades of bonanza, and of not so glorious ironies. Back in 1853 a Mexican who had worked in the Taxco silver mines passed through Gold Cañon and tried to tell the Mormon prospectors something: Pointing to some exposed quartz, *Bueno!* Waving in the direction of the mountain, *Mucho plata! Mucho plata!* But the lesson was lost in translation. Almost a decade later the same lesson had not been learned by as sophisticated students of making money as the Rothschild banking group. A Rothschild representative had secured an option on the Mexican mine adjacent to the Ophir and mining experts arrived from Europe to examine the claim. (This was the ledge that Comstock had traded for two mules.) The European engineers turned up their noses. "Rothschilds invest, they do not speculate," they said, declaring the claim worthless. The mine was returned to its Mexican owner, who in a few years became one of the richest Mexicans in the United States.

Of the original prospectors who let fortune slip through their fingers like stardust, only Old Virginny could be said to have died happily since he was roaring drunk and fell off his horse, killing himself while feeling no pain. Attempting to capture the almost hilarious pathos of the Virginia City pioneers, Mark Twain wrote in his western memoirs that Alvah Gould, half-owner of the claim that later produced millions as the Gould & Curry Mine, "sold out for a pair of second hand government blankets and a bottle of whiskey that killed nine men in three hours, and an unoffending stranger who smelled the cork and was disabled for life." Twain had learned in his *Territorial Enterprise* days that there is no compelling need to let the facts get in the way of a good story, although in this case the facts are almost as good, or sad, as the fiction just quoted: Alvah Gould actually sold his claim for $450 to the acquisitive George Hearst and lived out his days running a peanut stand in Reno.

H. T. P. Comstock, who gave his good name to the lode and had $11,000 to show for it, spent that sum and more bribing back a young Mormon wife who kept "trespassing" off with other men and establishing splendid dry goods stores in Carson City and Gold

THE LOSERS

Hill, which he ran with a heart as big as all outdoors. Dan De Quille in the *Territorial Enterprise* described Comstock's entrepreneurial activities:

"He soon broke up on the mercantile line, losing everything. He trusted everybody— all went to his stores and purchased goods without money and without price, and at last his old friends the Piute Indians came and carried away the remnants. Comstock made them all happy, male and female, by passing out to them armfuls of red blankets and calico of brilliant hues."

His wife and property gone, Old Pancake left the Nevada Territory for good, wandering to Idaho and Montana in search of another Comstock Lode. Little was heard of him until 1870, when he was reported to have joined the Big Horn expedition. On September 27, 1870, lonely and despairing, the old prospector put a bullet through his head in the gold fields near Bozeman City, Montana.

In a letter from Butte City, originally published in the Saint Louis *Republican*, H. T. P. Comstock had the pleasure of writing his epitaph: "I am a regular born mountaineer, and did not know the intrigues of civilized rascality. I am not ashamed to acknowledge that."

Peter O'Reilly held out for more money than most of the original prospectors, selling his share in the Ophir for $45,000. Almost immediately upon receipt he began building an ambitious stone hotel in Virginia City and speculating on the stock market and soon the money was gone. He died in an insane asylum.

The only Washoe pioneer success story of the exalted genre popularized by Horace Greeley, is that of the washerwoman-seeress Eilley Orrum and Sandy Bowers, the affable muleskinner she took as her third husband. Their story is also the most memorable, if melodramatic, romance in the unsentimental lore of the Comstock.

It begins in the predawn mist on May Day of 1842 on a moor in Scotland, where little Eilley Orrum was performing a Highland rite. The child watched a snail chugging across her slate leave a curly silvery trail which, with some imagination, suggested certain letters of the alphabet. There was an E and an H, also an S and a B. Eilley, only fifteen but with matrimony on her mind, knew from Highland lore that the initials traced by the snail were those of her future husband. Eilley Orrum flushed with romantic fever that misty dawn. Her keen black eyes saw in the fog shrouds and whirls a vision of a castle her husband would build for her, a castle befitting a daughter of kings. In her fervor Eilley's imagination had skipped more than a few generations, as her family was descended from kings in the same way that Indians can be said to be descendants of Adam and Eve—remotely. This daughter of kings clutched her snail-tracked slate to her bosom and skipped to her family's humble cabin through the wet grass of the glen as if waltzing on a grand ballroom floor with handsome rich men answering to names beginning with S and B and E and H.

Eilley told her parents of her vision, but their reaction was as cold as an unboiled potato. Eilley single-mindedly resolved that morning to leave the shadow of home and pursue her vision in the clear light of another world. An itinerant Mormon missionary provided the means of escape. Eilley converted to the white gospel of the Book of Mormon and found herself sailing to America with a boatload of Scottish converts who had shrugged off the Presbyterian pall of the kirk to seek a secular nirvana in the strange-sounding place called Nauvoo, the booming Mormon city in Illinois overlooking the Mississippi River. As Eilley stood at the ship's rail staring across the boundless Atlantic, she seemed hardly a child at all but a tiny husband-hunter armed with the gift of prophecy. She knew with a calm inner certainly that in Nauvoo she would find a man with the right initials who would build her palace; Joan had her voices, Eilley had her snails.

In Nauvoo, Eilley was true to her snails and married Edward Hunter, three times her age, a prosperous Saint who had contributed the weighty sum of $15,000 to the Church. This haughty man, who supervised the harvests with the strut of a peacock, was also a Scot, although from the Lowlands, with whom Eilley could share their native joys of scones and bloater paste when such luxuries were available.

The Elder Hunter soon became a bishop, but life in Nauvoo was not all tea and biscuits for the Bishop's wife. The work was hard—scrubbing, sewing, polishing, providing meals for the Bishop's many guests—the same sort of drudgery that had befallen the poor relation of kings in her native Scotland. Nor was it consistent with Eilley's sense of self-esteem or fairness that all finery be devoted to God and that men make all the decisions. These were the Mormon ways, and Eilley soon wearied of them.

The dreary expanse of the Great Salt Lake provided no spiritual uplift for Eilley when the Mormons moved to this "promised land" from the Mississippi. The Bishop seemed disinclined to present her with the mansion of her dreams and was unable to bless her with the child she longed for. The last thread that held the marriage together was broken when Eilley discovered that the Bishop had been lying to her through his whiskers and secretly engaging in the Saintly practice of polygamy—with three young "nieces" imported from Pennsylvania and as far away as Scotland to join their family. Eilley stood up to her full five-feet-two; she had debased her royal heritage by marrying a Lowlander of such mongrel tastes that he would lie with his own kin! She marched out the door directly to the Bishop of the next ward, where she secured a divorce for $15 and then went to the barn and strangled a rooster in a fury of expiation for her sin.

Eilley Orrum went to work selling calico and shawls in Enoch Reese's general store in Salt Lake City and awaited a sign that would tell her where to find a more loving husband with the initials the snail had written. She boycotted the Saint's Saturday night dances where, she said, all the available men were looking for a fifth or sixth wife, not a first, while the women they already had sat complaisantly in the corners like sanctified harlots.

One spring day in 1852 a tardy Argonaut on his way to the California gold fields stopped in the store to trade some things for blankets and beans. As he dumped valuables out of his sack, Eilley's eye was caught by a hefty glass ball. The Yankee wanted two pair of shoestrings for it but niggardly old Reese would trade him only one. Eilley placated the customer by offering the two pair and telling Reese she would work an extra day to pay for the ball.

"It ain't worth a day," Old Reese said.

"I want it," Eilley said. She got it.

That dusk Eilley sat the globe on a square of black velvet she had filched from the Bishop's tabernacle and peered inside as the faint orange rays from the sunset on the lake lit the crystal in a warm golden glow. Eilley saw something triangular—a stone monument, or a mountaintop. She saw a broad green valley and a lake, not a sterile white lake of salt but a glistening lake of sapphire water. Here she would find her fortune and build her castle. Every night her black eyes stared into the "peepstone," as she called it, and every night she saw the same thing. The stone became stained with her tears as she wondered how long it would take Providence to send her there.

After much travail and one more Mormon husband, Eilley Orrum at last arrived in the valley of her dreams in 1855 aboard a Conestoga wagon with a party of Mormon settlers. It did not bother her that she was the only person who considered the Washoe Valley Paradise, for she could look up to the pyramid, a dun-colored mountain peak, that she had seen in her peepstone. This was her place, and she experienced a joy she had not known since fifteen years ago, when she stood in the mist on the moor and divined her future.

Eilley bade her husband build her a cabin in Gold Cañon, and then sent him packing off to the so-called Utah War of 1857, when Colonel Albert S. Johnston led a military expedition into the Utah Territory to quell what was by that time widely considered to be fanatical practices among the polygamous Mormons. The Mormon campaign never amounted to much in the way of military action but it effectively rid Eilley of another unwanted husband who did not measure up to the standards of the peepstone or the specifications of the snail. (His initials were A. C.) She got a civil divorce on grounds of desertion and turned her attention to the prospectors who crowded around her like lambs around a mother ewe.

Eilley did not mind cooking and scrubbing for the boys because she was doing it for herself not for Joseph Smith, and her peepstone told her that among these rough men she would find the fortune and the husband that Providence had promised her. So she cooked for the taciturn Grosch brothers and washed the blue black stuff out of H. T. P. Comstock's pants and mended Old Virginny's long underwear and conducted herself with such a cheery and wholesome demeanor that she became truly the belle of Gold Cañon. When the miners came to her with their hopes and fears she peered into her crystal and told them what she saw in the future.

Often a miner would trade Eilley a few feet on a claim for a month's beans and board. She had her little claims marked with piles of rocks made to resemble the monuments she first saw in her peepstone. Later men came to buy the land under her rocks, but the crystal told her not to sell. The summer and fall when the great selling fever of 1859 swept Gold Cañon, she counseled her boarders to hold out, but they did not listen. None that is except Lemuel Sanford "Sandy" Bowers, whom, it could be said, she counseled more than others.

For services rendered, a miner named Rodgers had traded Eilley ten feet of a fifty-foot claim that Rodgers, Comstock, Sandy Bowers, and two other miners had staked out near the crest of Gold Hill. One evening while helping Eilley with the after-dinner dishes—as had become his habit—Sandy was chatting about his Gold Hill claims and it became apparent that her ten feet were next to his ten feet. When they found out that they were neighbors, they decided to move in with each other.

They were a handsome couple. Eilley was a short woman, and if you would describe her as plump you would say pleasantly so; her fine Highland beauty's face rose with all the pride of royalty above her pedestrian body like a Michelangelo head atop a lesser sculptor's torso; her powerful coal black eyes gave the impression of commanding all that she took in. Sandy was boyish, thin, and slow-speaking, with an awkward grace about him, a man of obvious wit and talent who had never learned to read a word, a muleskinner who had taught himself about mining and was beating the experts at their own game; his face was as broad and open as the prairie and his smile filled it with the fresh warmth of sunrise.

The holy act of matrimony was rare on Gold Hill and the Bowers-Orrum union a popular one, so the ceremonies that began in the morning continued into the night, with the miners hand by hand passing a lightly protesting Eilley in the air up a line until Sandy finally carried her over the doorstep. Pistols were shot off in celebration and many jugs of tarantula juice consumed before the last of the wedding party was shoveled from the stoop and Eilley and Sandy went to bed in the cabin she had sworn she would never "sleep" a miner in. The new Mrs. Bowers slept securely that night in the knowledge that her new husband's initials were S. B.

Providence smiled on the newlyweds, and Mrs. Bowers winked back at the image in her peepstone. Their combined twenty feet on Gold Hill was a pot of silver taffy; the rich ore came out in gobs as the Bowers laughed at the prospectors who had ignored the peepstone's advice and sold out their claims. A man from San Francisco came to offer Sandy a fantastic sum, $400,000, for the twenty feet. Sandy was sorely tempted, but the peepstone said no. Then a miner who lived up to his name of Savage sued them, saying the Bowers' mine encroached on his diggings. While the lawyers wrangled, Eilley looked into her peepstone and saw a stone wall—no, not a wall—a fort! Sandy hastily built a stone fortification around their claim and hired men with guns to guard it. The guards stayed put until the court ruled for the Bowers, as the peepstone had predicted—but, as Eilley said to Sandy one night over a dish of roast rabbit (Sandy was not a demanding man, but he had demanded no more pork and beans), even a peepstone can't be too careful.

It was all worth fighting for. In July of 1860 the Bowers' claim yielded $10,000; in August, $15,000; in September, $26,000. Sandy wasn't much better at arithmetic than he was at reading, so Eilley interpreted the figures for him: a quarter million dollars a year, she said. Then Eilley saw something else in her peepstone: a mill. In a few months Sandy with the help of his muleskinner friends had erected a twenty-stamp mill run by a sixty-five-horsepower steam engine capable of crushing twenty tons of ore a day. Eilley took out her pencil again: at a charge of $100 per ton of ore stamped, that was another million dollars a year!

"We got money to throw at the birds," said Sandy.

The good-hearted muleskinner thereafter couldn't walk into a saloon without buying the house a drink and a chaser too, and it became as routine for him to grubstake poor souls as to shake hands. Eilley promenaded the dusty length of Gold Cañon wearing billowing silk dresses of green and blue with fluffy white tulle sleeves and big feather hats as tall as an ostrich. When a Washoe Zephyr snatched her hat away there was a reward of a bag of silver coins for whichever of the boys could race the wind to fetch it back. The mine kept pumping out silver, the mill kept stamping ore at $100 a ton, and there seemed no end to the money. Some nights Sandy would stay awake wondering how they could ever spend such riches. Eilley had some ideas.

The site for her palace was by the sapphire blue waters of Lake Washoe in the green valley of her dreams. No architect was necessary as Eilley drew the building from the images in her peepstone. It would be the grandest home west of Scotland. There would be tiers of open porches ascending on smaller and smaller levels topped by a flagpole, in the manner of a pyramid. The walls would be of the finest granite and imported marble, the floors carpeted in elegant pile, and the doors would have solid silver knobs with silver keys attached to silver keyholes by silver chains. Outdoors there would be formal gardens with majestic fountains and towering rows of poplars, while indoors tropical plants would flourish in glass-covered conservatories. Piped from the thermal springs where Eilley Orrum once scrubbed the blue black dirt out of the miners' clothes, hot water would flow from the mouths of silver-headed lions. The furnished mansion would cost half a million dollars.

It was agreed between Sandy and Eilley that they would travel to Europe while their palace was being built. There they would buy splendid things to decorate their new home and visit Eilley's royal relations. Sandy gave themselves a bon-voyage party at

the new International Hotel. It was the finest party Virginia City had ever had. Every available luxury of possible pleasure to man was packed over the Sierra from San Francisco—terrapin, caviar, imported cigars, and an ocean of champagne sufficient to float the British navy. One of the boys had struck it rich and nothing was too good for his old friends. The streets of Virginia were almost empty that night, while inside the International Hotel the scene was one of glorious self-indulgence with miners smoking two cigars at once and trying to toast their beaming hosts with three glasses of bubbly at the same time.

In the midst of this boisterous chaos sat Mr. and Mrs. Bowers, the calm center in a hurricane of celebration, as dignified and dressed up as a porcelain couple atop a wedding cake. Sandy rose unsteadily to quiet the boys and say a few words. He was splendidly dressed in black broadcloth and a starched shirt with diamond studs and shiny black pointed shoes that squeaked. He told the boys to drink up—there was plenty more where the last bottle came from. "I've been in this here country among the first that come here," he began, raising his thin voice to be heard above the roar of applause. "I've had powerful good luck, and I've money to throw at the birds." The approving miners began to hoot and stomp on the wooden floor and the click-click-clack of their hobnail heels could be heard far down the mountain in Six Mile Cañon.

"There ain't no chance for a gentleman to spend his coin in this country, and there ain't nothing much to see," opined Sandy. So he and the little woman were off to "Yorrup"—to see the Queen.

The Comstock's emissaries to the Old World sailed from New York to London aboard the *Caledonia* after an uncomfortable journey by sea and land across the Isthmus of Panama. In the hold of the ship were trunks containing a quarter million in specie and bullion, which the Bowers had brought for spending money, and a solid silver tea service to present to the Queen of England. Eilley turned up her nose at the goats penned aboard ship to provide fresh milk; she told a fellow passenger that where she came from, a better breed of goats ran wild on the hillside.

In London the Comstock millionaires bought the first thing they saw that wasn't nailed down. A nonplused hotel clerk drew up a bill of sale for the bedroom furniture in the Bowers' suite, and a large walnut bed and bureau festooned with walnut grapes along with a similarly decorated night soil pot that had serviced many an English traveler were shipped off to adorn the master bedroom in the Washoe mansion.

Eilley took out the silver service and polished it and asked directions on how to visit the Queen. She was told that the American consulate handled such matters. Mr. and Mrs. Lemuel Bowers of Virginia City, Territory of Nevada, in due course presented themselves at the American ministry on Mansfield Street, where the newly appointed ambassador, the supercilious Charles Francis Adams of Boston, laughed up his lace sleeve at this incongruous couple from the West. The ambassador by way of discouragement said that Queen Victoria was presently at Balmoral Castle in Scotland;

Eilley thanked him and said they would go see her there, and the Bowers were off before the ambassador could pinch some snuff to steady himself.

In the town of Braemar in Aberdeenshire near the white castle of Balmoral by the Dee, the rain of disappointment fell on Eilley's pilgrimage. The Scottish gentry were far more impressed with their countrywoman so recently rich in silver than had been the officious American ambassador, and were on the verge of arranging a visit with Her Majesty when Eilley heard terrible words come up in the conversation: Her Majesty received no divorced ladies. Eilley's black eyes had the shocked, helpless look of a doe shot by a hunter. She could not bring herself to lie, nor could she admit the awful truth of the means by which she had rid herself of the Mormon husbands. Sandy made their excuses and led her away by the hand and comforted her like the good man he was. To make Eilley feel better he bought her mother a new house.

It was to Paris to bury their shame, and an orgy of Christmas shopping that implanted the word Comstock in the Parisian vocabulary as meaning rich, crazy Americans. Eilley swept into the salon of the leading Paris designer of 1861, one monsieur Gagelin. Sandy watched uncomfortably from a velvet stool as Monsieur Gagelin spun a Cinderella web around his wife with strands of ottoman velour, China rose silk, black velvet, and other fashionable dry goods in periwinkle shades to put the rainbow to shame. They bought diamonds by the cupful and whole libraries of morocco-bound books for Sandy—who had yet to learn to read—and antiques to make a Sultan blush at the spending. The unfamiliar franc did not seem like real money at all, but soon they had to wire home for more money. Money to throw to the birds.

Before tiring of the sport they chased the elusive shadow of royalty through Europe, almost seeing Napoleon and Eugénie at court, barely missing the coronation of Victor Emmanuel in Italy. Everywhere the Bowers went they spread the Comstock wealth: to a roadside sculptor in Florence, a commission to cast mantelpieces for their mansion; to a silver-tongued silversmith in Paris, a fabulous deal to make vases, candlesticks, table service, and even stairway railings from Comstock silver, along with an arrangement to ship the silver bullion direct from Virginia City to him in Paris; to a cabinetmaker in Edinburgh, an order for a small throne of walnut, straight-backed and armless, covered with fleurs-de-lis, a proper chair for the Queen of the Comstock to receive her guests in.

In London before sailing Eilley snipped some ivy from Westminster Abbey to grow up the granite walls of the Washoe palace, and that was the nearest they ever got to royalty. It was fall again when they arrived home to their newly completed mansion with a pile of bills waiting under the welcome mat. They had been gone almost one year, and had spent one million dollars.

The Bowers were without doubt the happiest millionaires to eat of the rich fruit of the mountain and the only ones among the original discoverers of its secret so blessed, but their story, as all true tales of the Comstock, has its bittersweet ending. A brass band was imported from Scotland to serenade the Virginia City gentry at the Bowers' new mansion, but the music had a sour ring in Sandy Bowers' ears. His mine had lost its vein while they were off chasing European royalty and Sandy in the next years could afford to spend little time in his wife's mansion. He spent nights on a cot in their drafty Gold Hill cottage and days frantically trying to eke enough income from the ever-diminishing mine to support their palace across the brown hills. With his illiterate mark he signed pieces of paper that eventually gave his bonanza to the bankers. Sandy developed a cough that the drinks in the Miner's Exchange saloon could not wash away and he died on April 21, 1868, with the dust of the mine and the mill clogging his lungs. Eilley was beside him in the Gold Hill cottage. Sandy, knowing the end was near, told his wife that he would not see her on the morrow. Eilley replied with all the authority of her vision that yes, he would, he would see her through her peepstone.

Creditors descended on the Widow Bowers like locusts. She began to sell off her treasures to save her palace, but when she took the king's ransom of the silver objects that had been cast in Paris to the appraisers they told her that the lot was worthless. It was not solid silver but silver plate; the miscreant in Paris had cheated them.

The mortgage holders on the mansion, unable to find a buyer for such an extravagance, settled on selling off the furniture and property by means of a raffle. Again the luck of the Scots was with Eilley as she bought a thousand tickets herself with her last funds and to the bankers' dismay drew the winning ticket; she had won back her palace fair and square, clear and free.

That night Sandy appeared to her in the peepstone and told her to make their home into a resort to make ends meet, and, precursing the fate of impoverished royalty of a later era, the Queen of the Comstock opened her home to the paying public and lost not one shred of dignity in the process. Sandy's library became a bar, and bottles stood where the morocco-bound books once were. Eilley received the curious from her throne in the second-floor parlor and gave peepstone readings to those with the price. She reigned supreme over this dominion and to her title of Queen the newspapers gradually added that of "Seeress of the Washoe" because her predictions by and large came true.

She saw in her peepstone the two great fires that ravaged the town, and when she accurately predicted the Great Bonanza at the north end of the lode even the scientifically inclined *Territorial Enterprise* acknowledged her "gift of second sight." Eilley Orrum Bowers died on November 15, 1903, predicting that there was yet one more great bonanza to come on the Comstock Lode, but she expired before anyone could ask her where or when.

The "Call to Washoe" of '59 was as unlike the Gold Rush of '49 as a silver rush can be. The Washoe was not the lush and invigorating country of the mother lode; it was more like an upper level of hell. The throngs of silver-seekers who mounted the old emigrant trail from Placerville, passing the pack trains of California-bound mules weighted down with Washoe ore going in the other direction, had the experience of seeing nature at its finest in the verdant High Sierra. But when they descended into the Washoe their faces fell at the first glimpse of their destination—the inhospitable pyramid called Sun Mountain—staring rudely down at them in a harsh majesty from far above the Carson River.

The Rush to Washoe began in earnest in autumn, after the first bars of silver bullion minted from Washoe ore appeared in San Francisco bank windows. It was propelled as much by caution as by greed. The gruesome lesson of the Donner Party taught the mortal peril of the Sierra in winter, and every man who wanted to go to Virginia City wanted to get there before snow fell. And thousands wanted to go. Most came on foot, some on crutches, many on mules or horses, and a few among the well-to-do by stage or covered wagon. The wilderness road became impossibly crowded—at its broadest two wagons could squeeze past each other but often the trail was a narrow path falling away a thousand feet or more on one side. And it was littered with the residue of men in too much of a hurry—jettisoned backpacks, discarded frying pans, empty bottles, broken wagons, dead horses. The Rush continued even into winter when hundreds of prospectors managed to negotiate the snow-packed passes to join the motley congregation of some ten thousand adventurers already camped on the side of Sun Mountain.

There had been ample warning not to come. The San Francisco newspapers had discouraged such an hysterical exodus even as it occurred before the editors' eyes. Failed, footsore Washoe refugees pushing home against the humantide flowing over the Sierra advised their replacements to turn back. The Cassandras of Carson City warned of the hellhole called Virginia City that lay ahead—of poisoned water, of starvation, of random murder in the streets. But few men who had undertaken the journey could tear themselves from the pull of the Big Magnet ahead.

Few were prepared for what they encountered. Since the Almighty doomed the outcasts of Eden to toil, no scene of labor has been so dismal as that which greeted the traveler upon crossing the Divide into Virginia City. The stench of sulfur and rotting garbage hung about the town that was called Virginia. As prospectors toiled under a broiling sun, lizards, horned toads, and rattlers scurried from their path. Near-naked Indians and men in frock coats wandered through the dirt streets of the tent town. With the coming of snow and the icy blasts of the winter Washoe Zephyr, tents afforded scant protection from the elements and the boys were forced to seek haven inside Sun Mountain itself. By the end of December, the mountainside was spotted with the stovepipes of prospectors who had burrowed into the soft rock surface that lay under the gray Washoe snow. Dan De Quille described the mountain in winter as resembling a giant face smoking many pipes. The fires in the makeshift wood stoves were sparse, for before winter's end the slopes of Sun Mountain had been stripped of all brush and trees for firewood. Talk around the fires was of the great days that would be coming in the spring; meanwhile the boys attempted to mine as best they could by digging little tunnels into the mountainside and hacking away at its innards, protected from the howling Washoe Zephyrs. There was little to do that winter except talk. By January mountain passes were blocked to all save jackrabbits and even Virginia City's monumental supply of booze ran out. Flour went to $80 a sack and miners began feeding their mules old playing cards for supper.

With spring came flash floods that washed away the pioneer mine workings at Gold and Six Mile canyons. Many of the boys who had suffered through the winter were ruined overnight, only to begin the next morning with stoic cheer that was characteristic of the Comstock miner. By March of '60 the Rush to Washoe was on again, but this time the silver hunters had to slosh over the damp Sierra and leapfrog mudholes that had swelled to ponds blocking the Washoe trail.

The spring brought new problems. Silver mining was new to the United States and there were no experts available in the territory. The men attempted to apply the tunneling techniques of placer mining, often with disastrous results. As long as a vein stayed steady—as did Sandy Bowers' at first—it could be pursued fruitfully; but once it turned down into the earth it became dangerous and almost hopeless to give chase. The task of extracting the ore from the deep ground was further complicated by overlapping and conflicting claims that made daily work a riot of disputes, wrangling, and violence. It would take the manipulations of cunning lawyers, enormous amounts of capital, and brilliant engineering innovations to open up the great silver pyramid. But try and tell that to men flushed wth silver fever! Judge Walsh, the night-riding assay expert from Grass Valley who beat the pack over the Sierra, had warned that the lack of timber, water, and technology on Sun Mountain would make deep silver mining impossible and that it would take extensive capital investment before the lode could be fully developed. But the miners were in no mood for such sober talk in the spring of 1860. They dug into the earth and took out what silver they could with no concern for the pitfalls that lay before them. They cared naught for winning the war; the battle was the thing.

The first great battle for control of the Comstock was fought on more hallowed grounds than that of money or mining—the fight was over slavery. Two strong men arrived on Sun Mountain in the winter of 1860. They were singular men, brave, clever, ambitious leaders among leaders, champions among champions. The two of them—much like two generals doing personal combat to decide which side would win the war while their troops watched anxiously from the sidelines—would settle the momentous question of the future of Sun Mountain, slave or free. William Stewart, a crafty frontier lawyer and sometime Yale man, represented the North's territorial ambitions for the Comstock against Judge David Terry, a fiery Secessionist from California who saw in the silver bonanza a means to finance the Confederacy.

Bill Stewart was a giant, yellow-bearded man. He came to California with the Gold Rush and went to Nevada with the Silver Rush. *The Gold Hill News*, published on the Divide, pictured him as "towering above his fellow citizens like the Colossus of Rhodes and having as much brass in his constitution as the famous statue." Fresh out of Yale, he spent nine unspectacular years panning for gold on the Yuba River before trading in his mining gear for a set of lawbooks. He passed his bar examinations and accepted the appointment to the post of district attorney in Nevada County in California. Stewart as D.A. was the stereotype of the two-fisted western lawman who dispensed a frontier justice backed up by twin navy derringers in his coat pockets. At his first trial, he was sent to jail for delivering a knockout blow to the opposing counsel's forehead, whereupon he sat out the night in his cell mastering the technicalities of the case. The next morning a cool and charming Stewart apologized to the court and won the decision.

Stewart's sense of humor extended to himself. One of his favorite stories was the time he met his match in a trial with lawyer A. C. Baldwin. To Stewart's great annoyance, the Court had sustained several of Baldwin's objections. He finally turned to the opposing counsel and snarled, "You little shrimp, if you interrupt me again I'll eat you." To which Baldwin replied, "If you do, you'll have more brains in your belly than you ever had in your head." The two became friends.

In Virginia City, Stewart dabbled in mining and excelled in law. The towering Yalie soon developed a reputation for honesty and bravery among the unschooled prospectors. He once hiked across the Sierra in midwinter—the same hazardous journey that took Ethan Allen Grosch's life—to borrow money to satisfy debts from a mining speculation. The leadership of the pro-Union forces on the mountain fell naturally into Stewart's capable hands. His strong sentiments caused domestic discord as his father-in-law was a former U.S. senator from Mississippi and Stewart's wife remained politically her father's daughter.

In Judge David Terry, Bill Stewart had a well-matched adversary. A former Texas Ranger who had fought in the Mexican War, the aristocratic Terry was a leader of the pro-Southern clique that dominated pre–Civil War California politics. He was elected twice to the state supreme court, the last time on the Know-Nothing ticket, which carried California in 1856. Terry was a handsome man of dash and splendor who was

FRONTIER LAWYER BILL STEWART

inclined to mayhem. He combined bravery and recklessness to a degree unknown in men of public affairs. His ascension to the bench did little to bank the furnaces of his soul. During a notorious street row in San Francisco in 1856, the Judge stabbed a vigilante policeman in the neck with a bowie knife, and it was only the man's miraculous recovery and Terry's exalted judicial position that save him from the vigilante's rope.

Terry was at once a gentleman of manners and chivalry and a rabid political partisan who preached violence and occasionally was its instrument. When he came to the Comstock he had already killed once for the Confederacy. His victim was David Broderick, the charismatic California senator who was a double threat to the Confederacy, both as a popular challenger to the Secessionists for the political control of California and as a brilliant leader of the antislavery forces in the U.S. Senate. Terry killed Broderick in a duel and thereafter was known as a "gentleman killer," but Broderick's death was, in reality, a political assassination.

Broderick's body was barely cold in its grave before the impulsive Terry rushed across the Sierra to claim Sun Mountain for the Confederacy. He thundered through Devil's Gate riding a magnificent stallion at the head of a private militia of southern sympathizers. The men in the tow of the pistol-packing jurist were all noticeably armed. Terry immediately announced that slavery was the answer to the labor problems of Sun Mountain. This opinion did not fall on unsympathetic ears among the Comstock miners, who had accustomed themselves to considering the Piutes and the pigtailed "Celestials"—Comstock for Chinese—as no better than slaves (one of the first rules adopted by the Comstock miners was that "no Chinaman can hold a claim"). In the saloons, the boys began telling admiring stories of how the Judge had run a tavern owner right out of the Sierra for daring to feed straw instead of oats to his horse.

In pressing his political position, the renegade Judge exhibited a cavalryman's innate understanding of tactics, of surprise attack and defensive enclave. His plan was no less than to claim the mountain and its riches as a war prize for the Confederacy. Stone-walled military command posts were hastily constructed at strategic points along the lode. Armed men peered from inside these "forts" down upon the tent city below as sentries marched with military precision and rebel shouts of "all's well" echoed in the night air over Devil's Gate.

Under the watch of Terry's guns, other memorable characters found their way up the canyon; most were to align themselves with Stewart under the flag of the Union.

A Jesuit father, Patrick Manogue, a former placer miner called to the priesthood, returned from a seminary in France to carry the cross across the Sierra and, together with the Episcopal brothers Rising, from New York, established the house of God firmly on the secular soil of Washoe. On the other side of the fence, theologically speaking, "Baron" Charlie, a black-sheep descendant of royalty, introduced the boys at the crude

Comstock gaming tables to the drama of high-stakes play, while a lady from New Orleans revealed the pleasures of even finer sport. She was Julia Bulette, who established in Virginia City the first Parisian-style whorehouse in the American West. In the process she won a permanent place in the hearts of the men who were more than customers to her. Julia Bulette, rumored to be a Union sympathizer, was also part Florence Nightingale.

"The Soiled Dove of the Comstock," as she came to be known, ministered to the sick and often provided grubstakes for the down-and-out. Julia's sanctum, with its exaggerated manners and French champagne, was the lone island of decadent civilization in the demented, stinking hellhole of Virginia City. With Julia functioning, turn-of-the-decade Nevada was no longer entirely a desert outpost of misery and carnage; her crystal chandeliers hung like sparkling diamonds over her world of voluptuous talk and soft furniture. The boys loved her.

And the boys were to gain leaders, and villains too. Big Tom Peasley, a dashing fireman late of New York City and San Francisco crack fire-fighting regiments, rallied the town in inspired fashion against the Secessionists, inflaming the boys with the glory-be of Abolition. On the darker side, the so-called Big Chiefs, vicious murderers of the stripe of "Bad Sam" Brown, drifted in to prey on innocent inebriates. Under his slouch hat, Bad Sam was as filthy as a wart hog; he often crowed of "having a man for breakfast." It is the fantastic truth that one night he killed a helpless derelict in a saloon and cut out the poor creature's heart and then curled up and went to sleep on the floor, which was still wet with the blood of his victim. There was great rejoicing in the saloons of Virginia City the evening Bad Sam was gunned down in an ambush near Van Sickles Tavern in nearby Genoa.

While Judge Terry and his Secessionists consolidated their position on the Divide, William Stewart was consolidating his law practice in the tent city below. Stewart specialized in mining disputes, and he was making a great deal of money. Estimates at the time were that upwards of ten million dollars in legal fees were squandered in mining suits. As his fortunes increased, Stewart became more cautious in the use of his pistols, arming himself instead with the weapons of compromise and litigation. Stewart dreamed of statehood for Nevada and a political career, but always his fantasies were contaminated by the swashbuckling presence of Judge Terry. Terry, for his part, was also in no hurry to get shot at. He, of course, was not above a little violence if his military position was in jeopardy. When two black Irishmen (both called Fenian in the inexact news accounts of the day) tried to jump his forts and stake out a section of the Judge's territory, Terry and his bully boys waded in and knocked them cold. But when George Hearst sent Tom Andrews, a Kentuckian with a well-earned reputation for violence, to run Terry off his property, the southern commander retreated to the higher ground of his remaining two forts, saying he did not "want" Hearst's prop-

JULIA BULETTE

BAD SAM BROWN

erty. For Terry it was better to fight another day on more defensible ground and for bigger stakes—and, certainly, before a larger audience. For Terry loved the drama of a big battle. And big battles were soon to come.

In early May of 1860, the tent city throbbed with excitement over a great boxing event featuring the miners' beloved "Benecia Boy," a former blacksmith from the California mining camps who was fighting a lad in a ring on the other side of the world in Harnborough, England. While the boys anxiously awaited the pony express to arrive with word of their former comrade's victory, "Pony Bob" Halsam, who had replaced Snowshoe Thompson as mailman, was streaking past Devil's Gate with news that was even more compelling. The boxing match was momentarily forgotten as the miners piled out of the saloons to gaze in shock at the sight of Pony Bob's bloody face gasping

at them over the flanks of his foaming mustang: Piute Indians had massacred three men and then burned down Williams' Station forty miles to the east. "Five thousand braves" were on the warpath, the bloodied messenger said. The savages were riding on Six Mile Cañon!

Virginia City became gripped by a paranoia that far outweighed the gravity of the crisis. Stewart wired Governor Downey in California for arms. His law partner, Henry Meredith, immediately formed a vengeance "Committee of Five," which was to number considerably more than that. Further up on the hill, Terry's sentries scurried about in panic to incessant, almost comic opera drumbeats, while a little volunteer army was fashioned in front of the saloons on C Street. The women of Virginia City, including Eilley Orrum and Julia Bulette, were ceremoniously escorted to Peter O'Reilly's half-finished stone hotel for safety. By afternoon, the citizen army rode out toward Williams' Station to join other hastily activated military units under the commands of

Captain R. G. Watkins, one-legged veteran of filibustering expeditions in Nicaragua, Major Frederick Ormsby, U.S. Marshall John Blackburn, and President James Buchanan's new appointee, Territorial Judge John Cradlebaugh. It was a festive departure not unlike that of little boys on parade at military school. The Indians, seasoned guerrilla fighters, silently watched from the hills as the noisy amateur soldiers marched to Williams' Station and beyond to the Piute sacred burial ground at Pyramid Lake.

Four days later, on Sunday, May 13, an alkali-stained horseless cavalryman staggered up Six Mile Cañon with news of ambush and the deaths of seventy-six miner-soldiers. Throughout that ghastly Sunday other stragglers supplied mournful details of the disaster.

The battle had started in treachery born of panic: a miner had opened fire on the Indian chieftain's negotiating party, which had ridden out seeking peace. As the Virginia City cavalry chased the Indians into Pyramid Valley, the Piutes had surprised them, screaming down from the steep walls of a narrow pass. Most of the troops had panicked and run, only to be hacked apart by the ferocious braves. A courageous few stayed to fight, led by Stewart's law partner, Meredith. They fell one by one, until only two were left. When his companion begged him to retreat, the wounded Meredith ordered his comrade to leave without him. Then Meredith turned his handsome face to accept a hundred arrows. Later, his pinioned, lifeless body gave up its scalp.

The fallen Meredith provided a rallying cry for the inevitable counterattack that would come from Sun Mountain. Martial law was declared on the Comstock. Governor Downey dispatched California's crack Sierra Battalion to the rescue, and under Colonel Jack Hayes, 1000 professional soldiers marched over the mountains into Virginia City. Captain Edward F. Storey, a veteran of the Mexican War, organized the Volunteer Virginia Rifles. Militiamen poured lead and even silver into bullet molds; a homemade cannon was mounted to defend Gold Hill. When U.S. Infantry arrived with howitzers from the San Francisco Presidio, the expeditionary forces marched out to revenge Henry Meredith. At the site of the Pyramid Lake Massacre, the troops found what was left of him. The Virginia Rifles lifted the corpse onto a stretcher, covered the grisly remains with a military cape, and carried the makeshift bier of the hero into the Battle of Pinnacle Mountain. The enraged, heavily armed professional soldiers drove the outnumbered Piutes into the wasteland of the desert. In the final skirmish Captain Storey was shot through the lungs. The grateful militiamen named Virginia City's environs Storey County in his memory. Chief Winnemucca's Piute braves were never again to threaten Nevada's mining camps, and the irony is that they never did. The Williams' Station Massacre was discovered to be the arguably justifiable vengeance of another tribe whose squaws had been imprisoned and abused by white men. The Piutes were never involved. The white man had been too quick to shoot first and ask questions later.

After the funeral ceremony for Captain Storey was over, Colonel Hayes rode down Gold Cañon to prepare for the departure of his California Expeditionary Force. There was no arsenal in the territory, and the commander looked for a fortified location—under a responsible authority—in which to store his surplus eighty stand of arms. Judge Terry, a man well versed in the care and use of firearms, was fortuitously present with a solution to Hayes's problem. When the Sierra Battalion broke camp for the Presidio, Terry's quartermasters took the weapons for safekeeping in their encampment above Gold Hill. California had armed the Confederacy.

As the Piute war fever ebbed, Virginia City returned to the hard business of silver mining. It proved to be almost as dangerous as Indian fighting. The first mining shafts—"coyote holes" at least 100 feet deep that miners were lowered into by hand-operated winches—were replaced by timber-supported square shafts and tunnels boring deep into the mountain. Miners descended to the depths with the aid of noisy steam-powered hoisting machinery. They frequently were escorted underground by armed guards. Subterranean battles over connecting mine shafts were common, and when fisticuffs and pickaxes failed to settle just whose ore belonged to whom, professional fighters were brought down into the mines to do the dirty work. Stink bombs were often used by the losing side to drive the victors from their spoils, while topside Virginia City residents walked the streets with handkerchiefs to their noses to fend off the rotten-egg stench of sulfur gases drifting up from below.

When J. Ross Browne, the world traveler and distinguished early resident of Oakland, visited the Washoe mining camp he was flabbergasted by the multifarious ledges being developed almost on top of one another. He attempted to map the overlapping claims, but "results of an actual survey are precisely the same as those produced by a bundle of straw well inked and pressed upon a piece of paper." The mind-boggling confusion, litigation, and violence that marked the development of Comstock mining was abetted by a "law" of the early miners that said a man followed his vein to wherever it went; whether it went into his neighbors' backyard, or to China, was not taken into consideration by the unsophisticated miners. "If we were to give laws to a nursery, we should give them childish laws," wrote the poet Goldsmith.

The original Comstock claims were for possession of the surface ground in the tradition of placer-mining claims. But once the ore was removed from the partially decomposed surface quartz and the mine owners realized their vein or "ledge" continued into the earth, they claimed all the "dips, spurs and angles" of the vein. Comstock mining law thereafter became a chaotic history of underground collisions between com-

Overleaf:
UNDERGROUND BATTLE IN THE MINES

peting ledges and arguments of the chicken-or-the-egg variety about which came first. The great courtroom battle that began the seemingly endless and hideously expensive Comstock "ledge" litigation was fought between the forces of North and South for control of the mountain.

The menacing presence of Judge Terry's armed miners in their fortified hillside claims overlooking the wooden housings of the mines stretching from Gold to Six Mile canyons contributed immeasurably to a growing sense of desperation on the part of the pro-Union mine owners below. That this tension was well founded is evident from any inquiry into the condition of law and order under the notoriously corrupt territorial governments of the West. In the wilderness of the Washoe, the law was less an object of jurisprudence than of commerce—something to buy or sell. If you could not bribe the jury you bought the judge, and an honest judge was considered to be one who, when bought, stayed bought. (Sam Davis, in his history of Nevada, documents the Aesopian story of one Comstock judge who let it be known that his opinion in a case at bar could be purchased by the first person to deliver $10,000 in gold to his house that evening. Toward midnight a litigant knocked at the judge's door holding a forty-pound sack of gold pieces. The judge's wife opened the door in her nightgown and whispered that His Honor was asleep. When the man said that he had brought the money, she volunteered to receive it. The woman of the house gathered up her nightgown in the manner of gathering an apron and as the visitor poured out the contents of his sack the weight of the coins tore off her nightgown and left the judge's wife standing nude in the doorway with gold pieces scattered about her.)

Virginia City juries were selected in cavalier fashion; panels might consist of all cross-eyed men or of men all over six-foot-six. Even if an honest judgment was won it was the devil's own game to enforce it, as the Comstock at that time had but one U.S. marshall amid a sea of desperadoes who hired out their guns to any cause.

Indeed the very lawlessness of the Washoe was the reason for the appeal of Terry's Secessionist cause to Comstock citizens who hankered for the rule of order. They were insulted by being ineffectively governed by the nondrinking Mormons of the territorial capital of Salt Lake City and had begun to despair of getting redress from distant Washington, D.C. Confederate government or Union government, the Washoe wanted *some* government, and soon. There were rumors that Jefferson Davis had designated Judge Terry Confederate Governor of the Washoe. And rumors that California might secede from the Union; hell, all the Comstock had to do was secede from the Mormons! The boys watched Judge Terry to see if he could make his law stick.

Mark Twain arrived in Virginia City in time for the North-South struggle. He expressed the ambivalence felt by many on the Comstock: "I am perfectly willing to fight for either the U.S. or the Confederacy, but this damned uncertainty as to which side I am on is killing me with anxiety." A majority of the mine owners had at least vague Union sympathies and thereby opposed Judge Terry on ideological grounds. They were, however, far more opposed to him on practical grounds: the son of a bitch was on their land. Millions were at stake, and Terry and his well-armed Secessionist partisans seemed capable, if the tides of opinion rolled their way, of confiscating the entire Comstock in the name of Jefferson Davis.

When this understanding of the pocketbook implications of the politics of slavery dawned on the Comstock, the mine owners, with a renewed sense of Unionist fervor, organized to drive Terry out into the desert.

But there was a legal problem, and a knotty one at that, to be settled first among the Unionists. The new Gould and Curry, the Ophir, and the Mexican mines were tangled up in overlapping claims of angles and dips and spurs that butted into the adjoining California and Best & Belcher mines. To settle the ultimate question of who owned what so they could stand and fight together, the managers turned to Stewart, who was now president of the Washoe Bar Association.

Geologists, surveyors, and engineers were hired from San Francisco to establish legal perimeters between the crisscrossed claims of the Northerners. The lines were established with a maximum of difficulty. The united miners then became increasingly belligerent in their demands to run Terry off the mountain. Stewart looked up at the forts over the Divide at Terry's façade of guns and stone. He knew the aristocratic Terry, as a former jurist, knew that in the haziness of the law, his squatter's claim to the land was as good as the next. Even a successful military foray against the forts would not settle the issue. Stewart opted to proceed with caution. He wanted insurance. He stalled for additional time while more maps were drawn. Gradually, the pieces of Stewart's legal puzzle came together, and the master strategist confidently began to build his case for the epic litigation to come. North and South would soon meet on the battleground of *Single-Ledge* v. *Multi-Ledge* Ownership of the Comstock Lode.

The key to Stewart's strategy was acquiring Old Virginny Fennimore's long-forgotten claim up on the north slope of Sun Mountain. But Old Virginny's original scrap of paper—which constituted evidence of the first claim above Six Mile Cañon—was missing, and so was Old Virginny. Searching the town for the old prospector, Stewart finally found him drunk on the back porch of a saloon. Old Virginny was in no mood to budge. When Stewart tried to shake the information out of him, he spit in the lawyer's face. Stewart politely wiped the saliva from his shirt front. Still politely promising a free jug, he lured his victim to the gates of the Ophir tunnel and shoved him into a makeshift prison for the night. The next morning, after first demanding an eye-opening "hair of the dog" from his captor, Fennimore soberly guided Stewart and a party of Northerners to the site of his original claim. The old document was still legible— and Old Virginny handed over the claim that, unknown to him, was now worth millions to the Union cause. Stewart had his clients buy Old Virginny's claim for $7500. He would use it to argue that they owned a single ledge which ran through the Comstock and that the southern claims were actually on the Northerners' ledge.

There was talk in the saloons of a march on Terry's forts. Northern and southern fanatics glowered at each other across the Divide. Terry's men increased their vigil on the battlements. Everybody waited for Stewart, or Terry, to make a move.

When Stewart moved at last to litigate, Terry, always the jurist, agreed to a legal arm-wrestle. The case, officially known as *Ophir Company* v. *McCall et al.*, popularly named "the Middle Lead Boys" for a squatter named McCall and his Secessionist friends, was tried before Judge Cradlebaugh in September 1860. This test case would determine which side, North or South, would own the Comstock.

If Stewart's theory of one continuous or "single" ledge held up in court, owners of a "lead" could follow a vein anywhere until it petered out or ran into another ledge. Terry intended to show that silver ledges were actually separated by worthless rock formations, thus establishing proof of the many-ledge theory. Squatters like McCall would then have legal claim to their surface ground on the principle that ledges of ore could be legally divided into separate mining properties.

Stewart's theory of one giant ledge was a sophisticated variant of the old first-miner-takes-all law. He championed it quite brilliantly throughout years of vitriolic lawsuits in which his clients were always the ones with the main ledge. After it had made him a rich man, Stewart attempted to abandon the theory in favor of a more equitable determination of mining boundaries, but the fires of litigation were such that reason could not damp them. Eventually, the major Comstock lawsuits were settled not on principal but by merger or buy-out after the expenditure of fortunes in legal fees. The Ophir spent $1,000,000 disputing title to a small claim which it finally purchased for $50,000. The Comstock created more millionaire lawyers than millionaire miners.

The multi-ledge theory advanced by Terry was a variation of the infinitely more sensible Mexican mining law that established mining boundaries perpendicular as far down as the mine was dug. It was also the more popular, and populist, since it allowed in theory for the greatest number of mines to strike it rich; the more ledges, the more mining companies. It is a typical Comstock irony that Terry championed the better theory in the worse cause.

The week-long trial commenced before territorial Judge Cradlebaugh in a hayloft over a livery stable in Genoa, Nevada. The dulcet-toned Terry represented the Secessionist McCall, who was squatting on land claimed by the Ophir Mining Company. The courtroom was jammed with a hundred well-armed men. The two lawyers only increased the tension with an officious display of courtly manners which belied their deep-felt political animosity.

The jury fidgeted in the courtroom of hay. When court adjourned for the day, the bailiff shoved the sweating crowd down the ladder that led to the horse stalls below.

Grumbling armed partisans jostled each other along corridors filled with horse droppings. Long into the night, groups of men argued the cause of secession and multiledge, Union and single-ledge, under the soot-dimmed light of kerosene lamps. To make matters worse, or better, there was no friendly all-night tavern in Genoa.

Despite the temper of the crowd, Terry and Stewart were bent on playing by the rules of jurisprudence. To demonstrate the seriousness of their respect for the law, they bedded down for the night in the loft on equal-but-opposite sides of Judge Cradlebaugh's snoring body.

Stewart took the offensive after the ladder was pulled up into the loft the next morning. He revealed that during the delay created by his stalling tactics he had managed to cut a thirty-foot-long tunnel from the Ophir into the adjacent "Middle Lead"—and silver ore had been found all the way! A parade of witnesses then shuffled through the hay to testify that the Ophir and the Middle Lead were one continuous body of ore; each man swore that the ledge did not break up or divide. The facts supported the single-ledge theory. Stewart confidently rested his case.

Quietly, Terry rose to introduce an equally large group of witnesses who testified that a twenty-foot granite vein, called a "horse" by the miners, lay like an underground fence *between* the two claims. Their testimony seemed to prove the case for the multiledge theory.

When court adjourned for the day, Stewart played his trump card. Relays of horses were whipped into the night from Genoa to the site of the disputed vein in Virginia City thirty miles away. There, ten men and a surveyor hastily cut specimens from the tunnel that had been dug through Terry's so-called granite horse. By dawn, forty sacks of what was obviously silver ore were triumphantly placed in Stewart's hands. There could now be no doubt that Terry's granite horse was a fabrication and that the silver capillary ran continuously in a single ledge.

When court reconvened in the hayloft, Stewart busied Terry with parliamentary particulars while a surveyor dramatically emptied the sacks of marked ore in front of the jury. The hayloft erupted in confusion. Over Terry's objections, the jury passed the marked ore from hand to hand for individual inspection, while the crowd hooted and gave out catcalls like a music hall audience. Then, astonishingly, Terry waved his hand over the courtroom and abruptly sat down; he was smiling. Stewart had played his trump card and Terry would let it pass. He all but admitted defeat. The jury retired as the Secessionists in the crowd grew louder in their contempt for Terry's lack of gumption. It appeared that Stewart had carried the day.

Terry sat complacently throughout the jury's long deliberation with the hint of a smile still on his face. As the hours dragged on it became apparent that he had something to smile about—in spite of Stewart's proof positive, the jury could not reach a decision. It was hung: the vote was eight for single-ledge, four for multi-ledge.

As the disgusted Stewart followed the jubilant Southerners out of the livery stable, he noticed an ill-concealed, gleeful familiarity between the four dissenting jury members and Terry's partisans. Terry had stacked the deck: the vote was really eight for the North, four for secession.

Terry remained in his arrogant entrenchment in the ramparts above the Divide while his men, emboldened in victory, formed a Secessionist gang that they dignified with the name "Rich Company." One of them shot a man for nothing more than his Union sympathies, and the Rich Company militants were suspected of being behind the Southern highwaymen—Secessionist Robin Hoods—who in the name of their cause were robbing ore wagons bound for San Francisco. Then the surly Southerners jumped the claims of the St. Louis Company at Devil's Gate and immediately began to strip the surface ore from the ground before the owners' eyes. Stewart, as lawyer for the company, sought an injunction from Judge Cradlebaugh to eject the interlopers. Terry was now confident that he could buy or bully the law. He turned over his eighty stand of rifles to the gang, instructing them to build a stone fort atop Devil's Gate. Judge Cradlebaugh granted Stewart's injunction, and John Blackburn, the lone U.S. marshall, was faced with recruiting volunteer pro-Union deputies to assault the fort and eject the Southerners.

For a time it looked as if the first shots of the Civil War would be fired at Devil's Gate instead of Fort Sumter. The defiant Secessionists had almost all the military weapons on the Comstock locked up in their fort-armory, but Marshall Blackburn fatalistically prepared to do his duty. Then a dispatch arrived from Washington that froze both sides in midmaneuver. President Buchanan, a vacillating Northerner with southern sympathies, had removed the strongly pro-Union Judge Cradlebaugh from the bench, appointing in his stead a foppish former ambassador to The Hague, the Honorable H. P. Flenniken.

The frontier jurist did not take his dismissal sitting down. He appealed the President's action to the Territorial Supreme Court in Utah and announced that he would continue holding court until his appeal was heard. In this he was greatly encouraged by Stewart, who found Cradlebaugh's pro-Union, pro-single-ledge sentiments ideal qualifications for a judge. Terry for his part said he would bring no more cases before the deposed jurist and would support President Buchanan's new judge, Flenniken, who would hear the various matters in dispute with a more objective ear. Once it seemed there was no law on the Comstock; now it seemed there were two laws.

The new federal judge arrived in Virginia City, sweating under his alkali-stained frock coat after the long, dusty stage ride. The florid-faced H. P. Flenniken had barely unpacked his velvet suits and powdered wig before Stewart was at his door, asking the newest long arm of the law on the Comstock to serve an injunction on the Rich Company raiders, or suffer the consequences of armed conflict between miners supporting the North and the South.

Flenniken was a veteran of the diplomatic minuets of nineteenth-century Europe.

Out West he proved himself to be a cameleon of etiquette. After agreeing to Stewart's injunction, he retired for the night, only to emerge the next morning with a fresh point of view; some romantic souls said Judge Terry had appeared to him in a dream; the more realistic said the judge had visited him in person that night and reminded him of his sponsor's southern sympathies. At any rate, Flenniken had no recollection of his conversation with Stewart; there would be no injunction.

The victorious Terry went to San Francisco on business. The pony express the next day brought news from Salt Lake City—the Supreme Court had overturned President Buchanan's appointment. Judge Cradlebaugh was recognized as legally holding office, thus placing tenure of territorial judges above presidential whims and on equal footing with federal judges in the States. The fat Flenniken waddled about the crowded boardwalks of C Street and made known to one and all his resignation from the bench. Stewart moved immediately to effect Judge Cradlebaugh's order expelling the Rich Company, but Flenniken, always a man consistent in his inconsistency, a man who stood before the world as living proof of Mr. Bumble's proposition that the law was an ass, in this case a fat one, heartened the Southerners by changing his mind again the next morning.

Before an excited crowd, the former U.S. ambassador was denying his resignation from the Washoe bench in stentorian tones when Stewart angrily shoved his way through the clusters of befuddled miners. Big Bill Stewart had his dander up. He had had it with this fig. Literally taking the law into his own hands, he grabbed the old dandy by the collar and pulled him down to his knees. The frontier lawyer roared some extremely unsettling sentiments at Flenniken, which, as a contemporary historian wrote, led the judge to conclude that he was a "prisoner of war in a military camp." Stewart dragged the terrified diplomat off the boardwalk into the gutter and drew him close, jamming a derringer into his quivering belly. At that Flenniken surrendered to Washoe justice.

Stewart marched his hostage directly to the telegraph station. He was not going to let the chameleon out of his sight until the case was settled. Holding the sweating justice by his neck, the lawyer dictated six quick messages of resignation—in Flenniken's name—to the federal authorities. Flenniken obediently signed the original copies. Stewart held onto his prey until the messages were reported received and a heavily armed marshall's posse had arrested the Rich Company garrison without a fight. Stewart, olympian in victory, magnanimously defended the hoodlums of the Rich Company as "good citizens." They had been duped by the "usurper" Flenniken, the false judge. He recommended their immediate exoneration.

Overleaf:
THE COMSTOCK CELEBRATES A UNION VICTORY

Judge Cradlebaugh, newly returned in place of Flenniken, slammed his gavel into the hardwood of a makeshift podium and released the prisoners with their eighty stand of muskets onto the sun-splashed street outside the courthouse. The battle was over. The streets were strangely quiet, and the remaining groups of onlookers talked in low tones as the Secessionists rode off in the direction of Judge Terry's remaining forts.

Everyone waited for Terry to return from San Francisco. The hot-tempered jurist had already killed once for the Confederacy. What would he do to Stewart? There were whispers of a duel between the two men. Stewart kept a vigil in his office overlooking Six Mile Cañon.

Three days later, Terry arrived back from his trip and made directly for Stewart's headquarters. As Terry strode through the door of the law office, Stewart, securing his

derringers under his coat, rose to greet his adversary. Terry stopped him in his tracks. Stewart some years later, in an interview with mining historian Eliot Lord, could still recall Terry's exact words to him: "We were beaten deservedly by our own negligence, for we should never have trusted our general in the camp of the enemy. You have both commanders, and it is no wonder that our forces were routed; but it is too late to grumble now. The victory and the spoils are yours."

The unpredictable Terry had played by the fading code of southern aristocracy; he had bought a judge, and made a bad purchase; the fault was his.

He turned abruptly on his heel and departed down the mountain to the east—through the great alkali desert that flattened out under his horse's hoofbeats—to join up with the rebel forces forming along the Rio Grande.

The War between the States was over in Nevada. Except for shootings that occurred during several Secessionist saloon insurrections later in 1861, the Union flag flew undisturbed over the Comstock Lode. On October 31, 1864, Nevada was admitted as a state. Its vote for the Thirteenth Amendment officially abolished slavery in America.

The world's most elegant dump grew up on the chalky yellow slopes below Virginia City. Each day, thousands of oyster shells were discarded with a woodpecker's indifference in piles that grew to the proportions of Indian burial mounds. The conspicuous consumption of oysters in a mountain city four thousand feet above the desert suggests all there is to say about the fabulous high life that came to Virginia City with the dawn of the 1860s. The extravagance began with the workers and spread upward. The miner, filthy from a long shift underground at the silver heart of the mountain, wanted to wrap his grimy hands around a glass of finest crystal and drink in surroundings consistent with the fabulous wealth within his grasp below. The saloons, which became the center of Virginia City social life, were the rivals in luxury of eastern gentlemen's clubs. As the wealth of kings poured out of the mines, money seemed an inexhaustible resource, water in the kingdom of Atlantis, something to splash around in in style.

Optimism was a communicable disease in Virginia City and ostentation its competitive spirt. Miners who struck it rich followed the free-spending example of the Bowers like lemmings. Jerry Lynch, upon finding his vein in the Lucky Lady diggings, shod his horse with silver shoes and ordered a walnut bed with the headboard extending from the floor to the fourteen-foot ceiling of his master bedroom. The superintendents of the first bonanza mines—the Gould & Curry, Ophir, Savage, and Yellow Jacket—became gentlemen and capitalists in the same instant and built themselves fine mansions overlooking their workings. No expense was spared to develop the mines. Elaborate mill buildings grew on the surface to support the mine shafts that cut into the mountain. "Snake it out!" was the order from the San Francisco mine directors and the economic demands of the war increased the frenzy of activity to a patriotic fever.

The mine superintendents were proud of the surface manifestations of the wealth beneath their feet. Mine headquarters were studies in marble and polished brass. When directors and stockholders came from "down there"—as the Comstock referred

Opposite page:
THE INTERNATIONAL HOTEL, 1861

Overleaf:
THE "D" STREET DISTRICT

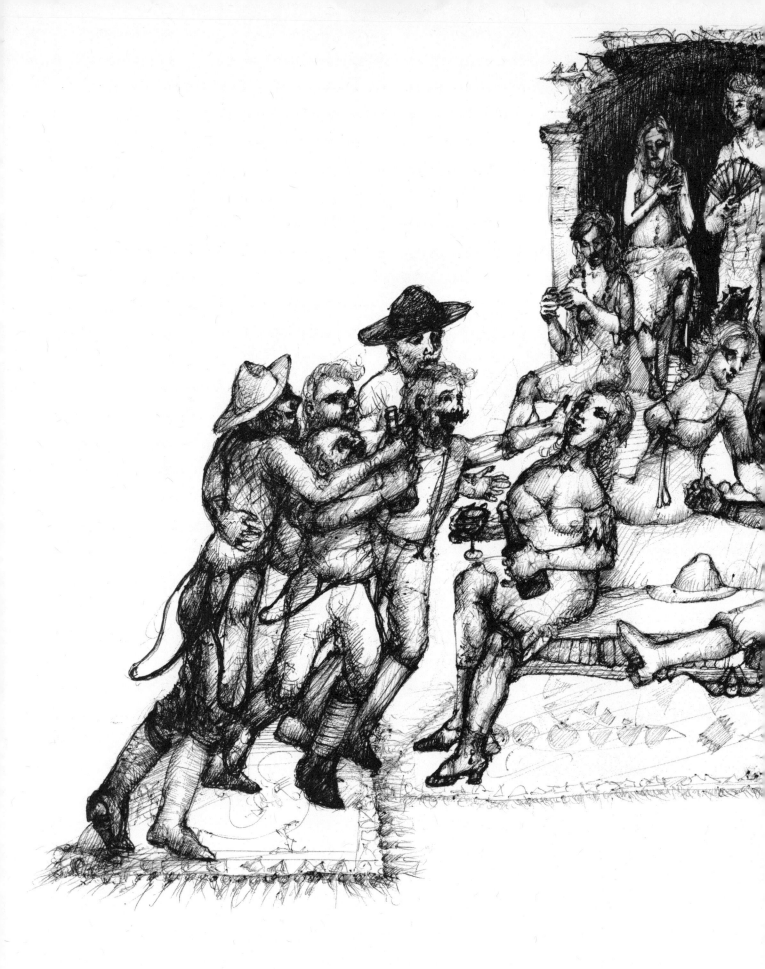

to San Francisco—they were treated as visiting royalty. They rode through the crowded streets in coaches-and-four rigged with silver harnesses, dined on oysters and frogs' legs served on silver platters, wiped their bearded mouths on the finest French linens, and washed down the feast with vintage Moselle with champagne and brandy for dessert. The six-story International Hotel opened in 1861 for the pleasure of visiting grandees and was known far and wide as the finest hostelry west of Chicago. It even had an elevator.

As Virginia City's terraced streets were cut into the mountainside, no one gave a thought to cross-traffic; the quickest way to get from one block to another was to go through someone's living room. The levels of the town developed along layers of caste and discrimination approximating those of our own day. C Street, the main business street, was lined with saloons, brick commercial establishments, and balconied houses with iron shutters. Most buildings had second-story balconies that left the wooden boardwalk below in shadows. Up the hill on A and B streets were the splendidly appointed homes of mining executives and well-to-do merchants, while the miners crowded into tent houses and makeshift clapboard apartment houses farther down the slope. Immediately below the main business district on D Street were the prostitutes' white cabins. Julia Bulette lived on D Street in a dignified cottage with flowers growing in the front yard. Beneath the whores, a full-blown Chinatown grew up on E Street, where ducks and salamanders dried on lines and opium dens and laundries abutted. Farther below the Chinese, near the oyster-encrusted dump, the exploited and vanquished Indians camped, living off the table scraps of white and yellow alike.

Everything but ice cubes had to be imported to Virginia City, and the High Sierra streamed with caravans hauling heavy machinery and luxuries into the mountain mining metropolis. Even the highwaymen had class. The most distinguished of their breed was Jack Davis, who spread a buffalo rug on the ground and treated his victims to champagne and cold chicken while his men picked their pockets and rifled the strongbox. The boys admired such style, as they admired any extravagance; one miner bragged of filling the water tower with imported champagne to quench the thirst of his wedding party. Virginia City thrived on what J. Ross Browne termed "an atmosphere of exaggeration." Flamboyant handbills were posted all over town advertising the latest excess—a battle between a bear and four bulldogs at Maguire's Opera House, or a Lady Godiva act atop a black stallion by the beautiful Adah Menken, the toast of Europe and the beloved of Swinburne and Dickens, who had come all the way to the Comstock to display her charms before the world's richest proletariat.

Down C Street each day Italian fresco painters hired to decorate mansions mixed with the Celestials in their pigtails, real Indians mingled with cigar-store Indians, and booted German engineers with muleskinners wearing the traditional Sierra stetson. Joe

Goodman, the poet who was editor of the *Territorial Enterprise*, watched this surreal parade from the copy room behind the red brick façade of his newspaper building on C Street. The *Enterprise*, founded in the Carson Valley hamlet of Genoa in 1858, had relocated in Virginia City early in 1860. Its daily bill of fare included the highly literate output of Rollin Daggett, a walking whiskey barrel who was part Iroquois, and the bowie knife-carrying William Wright, better known as Dan De Quille. These frontier journalists were tough and aggressive to the extreme, writing in a spirited exaggerated style that was well-received by the *Enterprise*'s ribald, grim-humored readers, the miners of the Comstock Lode.

For the muckers, their subterranean struggle with the earth was also a daily confrontation with death. The outrageous phantasmagoria of the *Enterprise* style befitted this fact of Washoe life. The *Enterprise* soon acquired a circulation beyond the confines of Nevada, both for its literary style, unsurpassed in the American West, and the hard, unquestioned knowledge of geology and mineralogy that made it the most informed mining periodical in the United States.

While reporting the blush of exuberance that was Virginia City in the early sixties, the editors of the *Enterprise* began receiving a series of frontier sketches postmarked from an anonymous prospector in Aurora, a mining camp 130 miles away. The copy was signed simply "Josh." The unknown correspondent described the Fourth of July oration by George Turner, the egotistical new territorial Chief Justice, thusly: "It was impossible to print his lecture in full, as the typecases had run out of capital I's." The writer nicknamed the Chief Justice "Mr. Personal Pronoun." Goodman offered "Josh" a job. Two months later, Samuel Clemens arrived in Virginia City by stage to take up apprenticeship in the sagebrush school of journalism.

"Josh" Clemens quickly acclimated himself to the exotic demands of the Sun Mountain reading public. He was an authentic American Original, and his columns had a wild and powerful imagination. On Groundhog Day, 1863, he emerged into the demonic sunshine of his art with his first report signed with yet another alias, this one to last forever—"Mark Twain."

Mark Twain, the developing journalist, owed the most to Dan De Quille. Behind the dry mask of the expert mining reporter, behind his long cape and wide black hat, "Dandy Quille" (as his friends called him) nurtured an acerbic surreal wit. In stories he called "Quaints," he loosed a barrage of deadpan science fiction in the pages of the *Enterprise*. De Quille's "Travelling Stones of Pahrangat Valley," which fantasied the discovery of peripatetic pieces of magnetic iron ore in southeastern Nevada, motivated German physicists to experiment with electrolysis and electromagnetic currents; with singularly Teutonic stuffiness, they addressed scientific inquiries to the "Hochvolgeboren Herr Doktor Dan De Quille, physicist of Virginiastadt," and could never understand the hilarity involved. Even P. T. Barnum was fooled, offering De Quille $10,000 to exhibit his traveling stones under the big top.

The best part of the story to De Quille's Washoe readers was the laugh that the "primitive" Comstock was having on the sophisticated outside world. Another De Quille hoax, a report of a giant windmill atop Sun Mountain as a sump-pump energy source, was judged feasible by a respectable Boston engineering journal whose editor proceeded to calculate its exact horsepower. His greatest fictional "news story" remains his report of "Solar Armour"—an ice helmet invented for crossing the scorching Forty Mile desert east of Virginia City. Fitted with an ammonia tank, the helmet furnished a cold vapor that neutralized the 117-degree desert heat and guaranteed the wearer a safe voyage to the Utah Territory. De Quille filed an eyewitness dispatch of the inventor's last trek across Forty Mile, which. alas, resulted in the demise of the genius. When a rescue party found the overdue inventor, he was seated on a boulder in the middle of the desert, frozen to death, icicles hanging from his body. De Quille solemnly attributed his death to a mechanical defect that refrigerated the man before he could shut his helmet off.

The *Enterprise*'s story was repeated as fact by many other newspapers, and when it was exposed as fiction the pompous San Francisco press was furious. The *Times* of London, taking a more relaxed view, proposed that Queen Victoria equip her imperial legions with this new device for protection against the infernal noonday sun.

The *Enterprise*'s brand of humor filtered through the polluted upper atmosphere of Sun Mountain like a long, low belly laugh. The boys in the mines loved it. Toiling in a bleached-bone desert landscape, they rarely bothered to separate truth from fantasy, and it seemed to them perfectly natural that a newspaper wouldn't either.

The defense of one's literary opinion in the late-night saloon world of Virginia City often became as hazardous as mining itself. Mark Twain learned this the hard way in the spring of 1864. While Virginia City was debating the misappropriation of $3000 of a "Sanitary Fund" raised for victims of the Civil War, Twain wrote in the *Enterprise* that the ladies who presided over the Sanitary Dress Ball in Carson City had sent the money to a miscegenation society back east. James Laird, editor of the opposition Virginia *Daily Union*, defended the ladies' honor under the front-page headline: "ENTERPRISE LIBEL OF THE LADIES OF CARSON." Laird portrayed Twain as a man "who conveyed in every word, and in every purpose of all his words, such a grovelling disregard for truth, decency, and courtesy as to seem to court the distinction only of being understood as a vulgar liar."

This was dueling talk. The code was clear on the subject: public retraction by Laird, or Colt navies at fifteen paces.

The young Missourian, in principle opposed to violence, in practice scared to death of it, sought to retire, but the editorial staff of the *Enterprise* over sufficient whiskeys convinced the reluctant hero of the necessity for combat. On the front page of the next morning's *Enterprise*, Twain denounced Laird as "an unmitigated liar and abject coward." This rhetoric was a gloved slap across the face. Laird's acceptance was not long in coming. The duel was set for the next sunrise in Six Mile Cañon.

A fiesty *Enterprise* pressman, Steve Gillis, was chosen as Twain's second. As Gillis attempted to instruct his neophyte charge in the care and use of firearms, additional lethal challenges poured into the newspaper's C Street office. The outraged husband of the president of the Sanitary Dress Ball Committee also demanded satisfaction, and the defamed lady's many friends promised horsewhippings in the unlikely event her tormentor turned out to be the survivor of the duel. The *Enterprise*'s star reporter spent a sleepless night. When Gillis rousted Twain from bed for some predawn target practice, his fingers shook like the leaves on a cottonwood.

The sunrise splayed jagged yellow rays around the silhouette of Sugarloaf Mountain down Six Mile Cañon and a spring breeze nipped at Twain's bony frame as he and his second approached the dueling ground. Gillis set up a barn door for target practice and balanced a squash on top to represent a human head. The two men were sighting down the ravine when the shock of the shots rang out in the still Washoe morning. Laird was already there before them, practicing *his* marksmanship. To say that both journalists were less than sharp with a revolver is to understate the facts. Twain could not hit the squash; he could not even hit the barn door. Then the desert walls were still and Laird's seconds could be heard advancing up the hill. As Twain sighted for one last futile practice shot, a mud hen flew across his vision to light in the sage thirty paces distant. In sheer frustration with his partner's ineptitude, Gillis whipped his navy Colt in line and blew off the bird's squawking head. The headless body flapped pathetically on the canyon floor.

Gillis could not have picked a more opportune time to kill a mud hen. For as Laird's seconds approached the dueling ground they saw Twain standing alone, gazing off over the cottonwood, with a smoking pistol in his hand and the mud hen flapping about on the ground. The spring air echoed with Gillis' gleeful shouts about his man's superiority at thirty paces; look what he had done to a hen in flight! Laird's men beat a hasty retreat from the rocky battleground and frantically informed the editor that his opponent was a better shot than Bad Sam Brown.

Laird canceled the duel and departed the Washoe in disgrace. Mark Twain was not far behind. He had no desire to face the line of avengers waiting to take Laird's place. And his old enemy, Judge "Personal Pronoun," had issued a warrant for Twain's arrest—for dueling. That night the curlyheaded bard sat slumped in the darkness of the racing stage that brought him over the Sierra to San Francisco and another kind of immortality.

Tom Peasley, the renowned mountain orator and founder of Virginia City's socially elite volunteer Fire Company No. 1, was a natural leader of men. Engine Company No. 1 had the spit and polish of Peasley's former New York Zouave Regiment back

east. He developed fine moral qualities in his fellow fire fighters. They were a handsome and colorful crew of sixty-four strong, romantic young men who constituted a powerful force for human decency on the Comstock. They drove the so-called "Big Chiefs"—cutthroats, ex-convicts, and ne'er-do-wells who had come from the hedgerows of California to plague the Washoe—from the Comstock and then disciplined the black-hooded law-and-order fanatics of Virginia City, known as the "Society of 601," when they began committing crimes in the name of stopping crime. When Fire Company No. 1 marched in perfect precision on their Sunday parades down C Street, their luminous, handsome features seemed chiseled in rock in the deep afternoon shadows of the Washoe Range. They were the Comstock's Finest.

It was entirely fitting and proper that Julia Bulette, the benevolent whore and humanitarian madam, and an honorary member of Engine Company No. 1, reigned as Queen of the annual Fourth of July parade of 1864. Holding a brass fire trumpet brimming with roses, her dark hair crowned with a golden fire helmet, she rode down C Street atop Peasley's prize—the magnificent red Engine No. 1 he had outfitted in New York. Behind her, the red-shirted heroes hoisted their company colors into the summer wind. They were followed by miners carrying patriotic banners lovingly hand-stitched in silk by the great whore herself.

That Fourth of July celebration was to be Julia Bulette's last parade. The following winter the "Soiled Dove of the Comstock," goodhearted mistress to a thousand lost souls, was strangled by a drifter for her jewels and a few worthless furs.

The hanging of Julia's murderer was the social event of the first half of the decade. Crowds of miners mingled with top-hatted nabobs and fancy ladies under parasols who washed little sandwiches down with champagne. Many a strong man had tears in his eyes the day that Julia's body was laid to rest on her beloved Sun Mountain. A band of bareheaded firemen serenaded one of their own with "The Girl I Left Behind Me."

Julia's death marked the end of an era on the Comstock Lode. The hallowed days of parades and exuberance, of frivolity and goodhearted laughter in the saloons, were soon to give way to the high stakes cruelties of bankers. Big money was already on its way from San Francisco, from Washington and New York, from London and Glasgow. And a whore could no longer be a celebrity on the Comstock.

Opposite page:
FIREMAN TOM PEASLEY POLICED THE COMSTOCK

Overleafs:
A DUEL ON E STREET; SOCIETY OF 601 VIGILANTES RAIDS A VIRGINIA CITY BEDROOM; THE HANGING OF JULIA BULETTE'S MURDERER ENDS A VIOLENT ERA ON THE COMSTOCK

Part Three

THE BATTLE OF THE TITANS

The westward dip of the Comstock Lode carried the huge vein of silver directly into the side of Sun Mountain. At the 300-foot level of the Ophir Mine, it turned abruptly around and resumed its true course in a forty-five degree bend backward like a giant hairpin, in an easterly direction under Virginia City. To follow this elusive vein through the great Comstock fissure—which was nearly four miles in length and over twenty-five hundred feet deep—ten thousand miners, boring beneath the earth, would encounter explosive gases, hot springs, hellish steam, and pockets of boiling mud.

In order to understand the gargantuan cutting and grinding process that resulted in the first bonanza, it is necessary to return to the surface workings of the mines as they appeared in 1860. At first, muckers at the original Ophir, Mexican, and neighboring mines were lowered in windlasses and buckets through small round shafts, which resembled ordinary water wells, into grimy chambers fifty feet beneath the surface. There they hacked the dark rock from the walls with picks. Soon timber-supported square shafts of two or more chambers and substantially constructed tunnels opened the holes to a depth of one hundred and eighty feet. A crude horse-winch device replaced the bucket system and pulled ore to surface stations where the $1000-a-ton rock was shipped to mills in the British Isles. Lower-grade ore, known as second and third "stuff," was set aside for future milling at soon-to-be-erected local mills.

Then, in the spring of 1860, the Ophir struck water. Dividends from Comstock securities were abruptly cut off from investors in San Francisco. The water level crept menacingly up the incline as the Ophir directors rushed up Sun Mountain.

Two men watched the floodwaters in the Ophir with more than unusual interest. Both were men who, to use an oxymoron, believed in impossible possibilities. It is one of the lessons of this history that Nevada silver rather than California gold built San Francisco and these were the two responsible more than any others. They were during their lives at odds with one another, barely friendly enemies; yet without their separate contributions San Francisco would have remained a grit of sand in the oyster rather than the pearl it grew into. It was entirely without coincidence that the two were the most towering individuals among the giants of the Comstock.

Adolph Sutro, a San Francisco cigar importer and merchant to the early miners, came to Virginia City in 1859 and saw what few men saw: that the only sensible and safe way to drain and ventilate the deep mines of the Comstock was to build a long tunnel into the heart of the mountain with an outlet near the Carson River below. Sutro, battling what by most mortal measures would be insuperable odds, would spend nearly two decades and $5,000,000 building his visionary tunnel that would prevent the Comstock catastrophes that were in the making—floods, cave-ins, and underground explosions from the yellow phosphorated gases that had lain in lower levels of the Big Magnet for centuries.

A compelling public speaker despite his heavy Prussian accent, Sutro possessed a genius for engineering and an equal talent for politics and propaganda. The Alsatian Jewish expatriate displayed a positively messianic dedication in accomplishing his impossible task—one of the engineering miracles of the last century—and then turned his genius to San Francisco, where he was a populist mayor who defeated the railroad trusts, a master planner, and an environmentalist *pur sang* who forested the sand dunes, saved the seals, and tamed the sea for an outdoor acquarium. He died shortly before the Earthquake and Fire of 1906, warning of precautions that the city must take against a great disaster to come, as he had warned people years before, back in 1860, of what had to be done to make the Comstock safe for men to work beneath the earth. Both warnings went unheeded.

The second man we must introduce was the nearest thing California ever had to a Monte Cristo. William Chapman Ralston was that rarest of things, a visionary banker, a Napoleon of finance who used credit the way generals use cannon. An indefatigable booster, civic builder, and party-giver, he put the bloom on the rose of California. He captured the treasure of the Comstock and freebooted it over the Sierra to San Francisco, where it financed a dizzying array of architectual, commerical, and cultural advances that turned San Francisco into a splendidly insular Atlantis of the Pacific—a city state that minted its own coin, minded its own business, sprouted an indigenous literature, developed frontier Medicis salivating for the arts, published more news-

Facing page:
ADOLPH SUTRO

Overleaf:
WILLIAM CHAPMAN RALSTON

papers than London, and drank seven times more champagne than Boston and twice as much coffee as New York.

Ralston beheld a vision with his piercing dark eyes: San Francisco as a great seaport metropolis, a new City of Light as beautiful as Paris, a financial center as powerful as New York, a Golden Horn of the Americas on the world's greatest bay that would someday dominate the entire Pacific Basin. His colleagues in the banking fraternity had mastered the art of saying no, but Ralston did not know the meaning of the word; to him, there were only varying degrees of yes. His vision encompassed agriculture as well as shipping, opera as well as the expansive architecture that is always the mother art form of a great city. William Chapman Ralston gave San Francisco its silver lining.

The agency for this vision was Ralston's Bank of California, which became the dominant financial institution of the West by plundering the Comstock Lode. But with grand ends such as these, Ralston saw nothing wrong with any means.

Perhaps the one means that Ralston did not, in 1860, consider using was Adolph Sutro's proposed four-mile tunnel. It was too expensive, too crazy. But still the floods were a watery tourniquet cutting the precious silver veins off from the arteries of the Bank of California. In desperation, the management of the Ophir embarked on a variation of Sutro's idea. On June 8, 1860, work started on a small drainage tunnel that would bore through 1100 feet of rock to connect with one of the flooded underground shafts of the Ophir Mine. Laborers toiled day and night for four months. Finally, at a tremendous cost, the water-filled chambers were drained.

Along Montgomery Street the San Francisco directors of the Ophir lifted glasses of fine bourbon as their stock soared at the news of a dry mine. Their delight turned into jubilation when, at 175 feet below the ground, the vein widened abruptly to 65 feet—the first bonanza.

The hosannas had barely subsided when a new problem revealed itself. The long-sought bonanza vein was not only broad but soft. As the miners began to work the broader vein, loose soil gave way and rock crumbled at the stroke of a pick. In the candlelit chambers, death was ever-present. Finally, the crude posts holding up the ceiling collapsed, burying two miners alive in the soft dark hole that had been the toast of bankers.

More posts, more pine timbers from the slopes of the Sierra were cut and hammered into the shafts of the Ophir. Soon the entire Washoe valley beyond the Carson River was being stripped, leaving a barren expanse of pine-stumps and scrub. Timbers were dragged from the Sierra forests, which lay twenty miles to the west. But it was not enough; the walls kept collapsing, and work stopped again. Engineers were afraid to proceed, their designs a mass of meaningless hen scratchings. Dividends were replaced by assessments to stockholders and an emergency meeting was called in November 1860. Ophir director William F. Babcock announced that a quartz mill operator in El Dorado County, California, might have the answer.

The man of the hour was an unknown, former German miner, Phillip Deidesheimer. His plan was to resupport the brackish walls of the Ophir with a revolutionary "square set" timbering that resembled the cell-like interior of a beehive. Deidesheimer opened up a third gallery of the Ophir and cut in silver some 215 feet below the surface of Sun Mountain to test his theories.

It is, of course, difficult for laymen, among whom the authors of this book are included, to understand the special mechanics of deep silver mining, but the reader may be aided by this description from Eliot Lord's 1883 classic, *Comstock Mines and Mining*: "Using his El Dorado quartz and gravel experiments as a guide, Deidesheimer framed rugged timbers together in rectangular or 'square sets.' Each set was composed of a square base, placed horizontally, formed of four timbers, sills and cross-pieces from 4 to 6 feet long, surmounted at the corners by four posts from 6 to 7 feet high and capped by a framework similar to the base. The cap pieces forming the top of any set were at the same time the sills or base of the next set above. These sets could readily be extended to any required height and over any given area forming a series of horizontal floors built up from the bottom sets like the successive stories of a house. The spaces between the timbers were filled with waste rock or with wooden braces, forming a solid cube whenever the maximum degree of firmness was desired."

Deidesheimer's experiment was a success. Swarms of miners reentered the Ophir chambers to lower depths in new-found safety where they "stoped" or dug out the first fortunes of ore from wall to ceiling across a sixty-five-foot-wide silver slab. And in the galleries of Deidesheimer's honeycomb, the hacked-down pine forests of the Sierra sheltered the busy bees inside the mountain.

As the miners burrowed deeper into the Big Magnet they inhaled a filthy, foul-smelling air. Candles burned with a faint blue green flame and at the deeper levels the rocks heated to temperatures of over 120 degrees. When the first deep mines were dug in the summer of 1860, huge canvas air traps were rigged like absurd sails above the mines to harness the wind and funnel it down processed cloth pipes to the men below. But when the shafts went beyond the 200-foot level, sail-powered wind traps proved ineffective and a more sophisticated ventilation system was needed. Powerful air pumps known as "root blowers" cost a fortune, even in Comstock terms, but they were the only way to pump compressed air down into the mines. Intricate piping systems fed the cooling breezes through twenty-inch openings to the shafts below.

William Ralston dug deep into his pocket to manufacture great pumps and blowers, patterned after the ones used in the English tin mines at Cornwall, at Donohue's Foundry, and his Vulcan Iron Works in San Francisco. The huge pumps were hauled across the Sierra by wagon. In the lower levels of the Ophir, stripped-down miners were doused with water melted from massive ice rooms. Each miner was allotted up to ninety-five pounds of ice daily, which melted like butter on a hot stove at the lower levels. Miners put on gloves to lift their red-hot pick handles. Strangers visiting the mines were invited to boil an egg in the thermal waters of the Ophir. One such visitor was Ralph Ingersoll, the professional agnostic, who allowed that after an overheated afternoon touring the tropical landscape that was underground Virginia he was reconsidering his long-standing belief in the nonexistence of hell.

The precious ore that was extracted with such difficulty from the ground created still more problems on the surface. The question was how to reduce the ore to its pure silver. The first answers were unsatisfactory. In the beginning, the mines used the primitive Mexican "patio process" to crush the second- and third-grade silver ore to spurs with the hoofs of little mules. The overworked Washoe Canaries brayed pitifully, their skinny sides heaving with sweat, as their masters drove and beat them in a never-ending circle over dusty patios of rock. The process was as monstrous to the animals as it was expensive. Soon bigger basins, patios known as Mexican "arrastras," were constructed and lined with greenstone and operated by men with great ugly hammers who beat the rocks in deafening cadence as a heavy, horse-operated muller or bucking hammer ground the third-grade ore to dust. Many arrastras earned $1000 a day, but it was not enough.

Sun Mountain became a New Jerusalem for engineers. Germans and English and Frenchmen came to study Deidesheimer's square sets and to gaze upon this unusual underworld city that rose, or sunk, to twenty stories. It was commonly said that you could walk the distance to San Francisco in the damp subterranean pathways dimly lit with tens of thousands of candles. The lean torsos of miners glistened with sweat in the eerie light of the honeycombed chambers and their picks cast animated shadows on soft blue black walls that held the treasure. An amalgam of salt and copper sulfate stained the work horses' tails and legs, turning them a bright green. These luminous animals decorated a fantastic landscape, like a painting of the Fauvists from the turn-of-the-century to come.

While mining experts from Germany lobbied for a costly and elaborate revolving barrel system of ore reduction, the owners stuck to their slow and tortuous patios and the unending boredom and unimaginative symmetry of the circling mules. Finally local initiative saved the day when two Comstock pioneers, George Hearst and his

Overleaf:
(1) INTERIOR CROSS SECTION OF MINE SHOWING DEIDESHEIMER'S "HONEYCOMB" STRUCTURE; (2) DEIDESHEIMER'S REVOLUTIONARY SQUARE SET "JOIN"; (3) TIMBERING AND HOIST, MINE INTERIOR

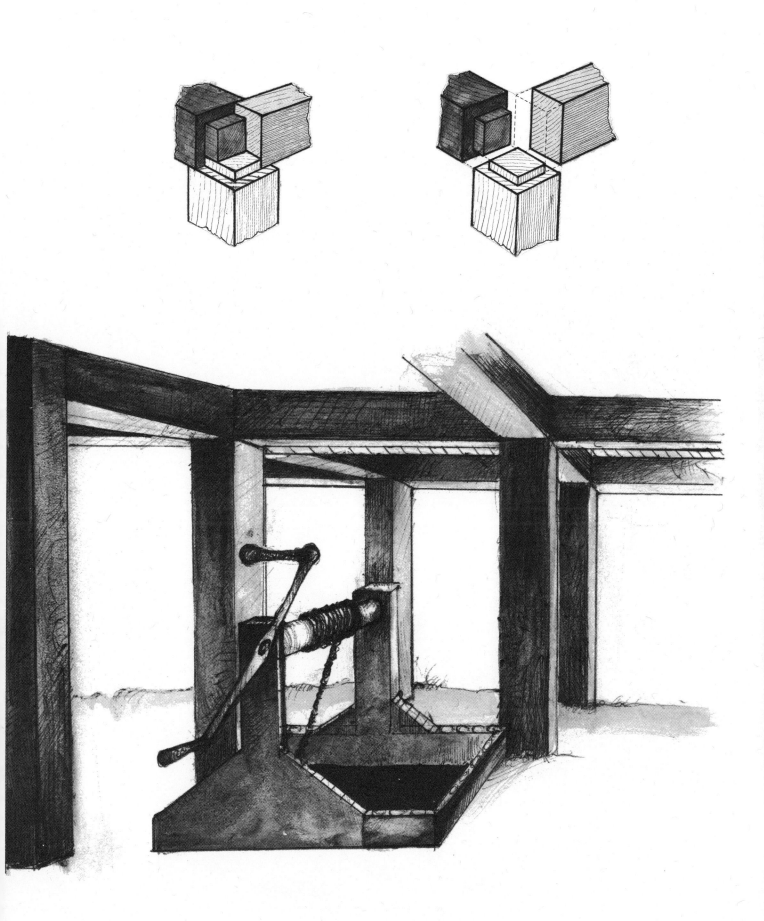

friend Amarin Paul, introduced a second mining innovation to the world—the Washoe process of "amalgamation," of removing and smelting crushed ore in giant pans. Hearst and Paul's Washoe Gold and Silver Mining Company advertised that it could crush rock for $25 to $30 a ton. Hearst and Paul committed their fortunes, pouring half a million dollars into castings made by Howland, Angel and King Company in San Francisco and the construction of a mill below Gold Cañon. Two months later, the finished castings were finally shipped to the mill, which stood near Devil's Gate where ten years before, John Orr, a Mormon wagonmaster, had found the first large gold nugget. Now a steam whistle shrieked over the rocky pilasters of Devil's Gate.

The mill's expenses were enormous. Nails cost $60 a thousand. But soon Gold Cañon echoed with the sound of twenty-four "stamps," or ironheaded wooden posts, smashing the rock like giant pestles. Huge iron troughs ran pulp and ore through settling tanks, amalgamating pans, agitators, and separators, leaving quicksilver and precious metal in a shining, soft amalgam in the pan. A fiery retort burned off the quicksilver, revealing the shimmering Comstock Silver.

The Washoe process became a triumph of science and sweat. Soon, the invention of a more efficient sixty-four-stamp mill encouraged a rush of mill construction, until the barren slope below Virginia City was like an enormous factory-town breaking the mountain silence with the cacophony of steam whistles. And sadly, inevitably, the clear blue sky, with its peculiar, razor-edged, saucer clouds, filled with soot. Atmospheric pollution had come to the American West.

There were other improvements of a sort. Mine owners had discovered a new beast of burden that could pack twice the load of mules. A curiously biblical look came over the cloudy tableaux of Sun Mountain as companies of camel trains, imported from Asia Minor, began carrying salt to the mills from Teal's Marsh on Walker River.

Loping in single file along the Divide to commands of their Turkish caravan masters, these alien beasts terrified the Comstock horses and Washoe Canaries, who bolted in terror at the strange scent. It thus became necessary to bring the camels carrying their 450-pound blocks of salt into town by night, along little-used trails and through back streets, to rendezvous above Virginia City's mill yards. And if a late-night patron of the saloons was occasionally startled by camels in his backyard, the animals themselves enjoyed the warm sands of the Nevada desert. But, according to Eliot Lord, their work as substitute pack animals for mules "was not a pronounced success, for they disliked to travel on stony mountain paths which formed part of the route, and could hardly be urged forward by blows and curses."

CAMELS ON THE COMSTOCK

While Adolph Sutro continued to talk about his tunnel to anyone who would listen, other outsiders were establishing crucial grubstakes underground. Among them, two Irishmen had come to stay. John Mackay, who was to be the greatest of the Comstock miners, began work as a mucker, laboring half-naked in the mines. He kept his body hard with austere living and he neither smoked nor drank. All his energies were taken up with the concepts, techniques, and practice of silver mining. With the same methodical precision that overcame a childhood speech handicap, he had become an expert boxer and poker player. Mackay had replaced his nervous stuttering with a slow and sparse delivery that made him a commanding presence even in his middle twenties. Later, when he was the most important of the bonanza titans, a clerk at San Francisco's Palace Hotel would describe Mackay to a visitor as "the one who says nothing and pays the bill."

Mackay was joined by the superintendent of the Ophir Mine, who listened carefully to his pronouncements on mining. James G. "Slippery Jim" Fair was the dark shadow for Mackay's image of sparse honesty. Fair claimed to have founded his career on other men's failures and became a manipulator without peer on the mountain. Slippery Jim was lured to Washoe from temporary retirement on a farm in Petaluma, California. From a family of mechanics he had inherited an enthusiasm for all forms of mining machinery. He was the only future titan who had, himself, operated a successful mining company—at Angel's Camp in California during the Gold Rush.

Two other Irishmen would complete the quartet of stubborn mavericks who would stand in mulelike opposition to Ralston's takeover of the Comstock. William Shoney "Jack" O'Brien, a Dubliner, came to California with the Gold Rush and stayed to lunch on luck. O'Brien would rise to wealth on the coattails of accident, never losing the common touch, while Jim Flood, a New York City lad, had taste and pretention that exceeded his station behind the plank at his Washington Street bar in San Francisco. Flood would trade his saloonkeeper's white apron for the frock coat of the financier in the firm of Flood and O'Brien and would one day brag to Ralston that if he ever poured drinks again it would be over the counter at the Bank of California.

Ralston had founded his Bank of California on profits from the Ophir and he continually touted his customers to "buy Comstock" in order to inflate his Virginia City mining stocks. But the San Francisco stock market crashed in the summer of 1864. The Comstock had come to a standstill once again. There was scalding water at the 700-foot levels of the Ophir, the Gould and Curry, the Chollar, Belcher, and Yellow Jacket mines, and the great pumps were clogged with steam and boiling mud. Lawsuits and injunctions wrapped the big producers in a morass of red tape. Mills were slowed for lack of ore from the mines along the Divide and hoists and pans stood ominously silent. The steam and phlegm brown soot began to clear over Chief Winnemucca's soft white valley to the east. But William Chapman Ralston didn't give a damn about clean air. He was going to be ruined.

The boys didn't give a damn about clean air either. They were after the big bonanza. They worked for a lordly four bucks a day, the best-paid miners in the world. They boozed up and down C Street on Saturday night, and they stumbled bashfully out of the whorehouses at dawn on Sunday mornings in time for church, blinking at the sunrise like hungover moles. The boys had come to work deep inside of this godforsaken mountain, risking their lives to cave-ins and explosions, fire and scalding floods, and that worst of all deaths, death by suffocation. Why?

Certainly not for four bucks a day and a few frontier whores. The boys had come from all corners of the earth to see an abstraction, the Big Magnet, whose riches were beyond imagining. How could they cope with such a vein of shimmering rock? It seemed to give off an ethereal, faintly luminous blue black light. You couldn't quite blink it out of your head at night, or drink it away. Yet at last here was the wealth of Solomon, of the Bible, under your own two feet. You could actually stand on it, the richest floor in creation, jump on it, pat it, hack at it, swear at it, piss on it! For one eternal moment in a lifetime it was yours, and in a strange way the Big Magnet had a life of its own, an energy that whispered to the boys of immortality.

So when the dreaded croak of "borrasca" or "barren rock" wailed out in the night zephyrs that swirled down Six Mile Cañon the boys were as despairing as William Chapman Ralston in San Francisco.

Old Comstock hands said the mines were through, petered out. They'd never get rid of the water. Already hundreds of former miners had rattled down the grade in covered wagons, searching the desert for new El Dorados.

Depression came to the Comstock. Stateler and Arrington, Ralston's banking correspondents in Virginia City, failed, leaving the Bank of California obligated to take care of the payrolls for irate teamsters and oreman. The bank's reserves were dwindling. Ralston sent a newly found Iago, William Sharon, to deal with the crises.

The steely eyed Sharon, Quaker-born and farm-bred, was a cool-eyed, dandified little man, a graduate of Ohio's Athens College, who had parlayed conservative real estate investments into a comfortable estate when he was stricken with "Comstock Fever." He had bet $150,000, his savings of fourteen years, on mining stock and lost it all, victim of a stock jobber's swindle. Using a friendship with Colonel Fry, Ralston's father-in-law, as an introduction, Sharon hocked his real estate to the Bank of California to

Overleaf:
HALLUCINATION OF THE MINER

pay his debts and accepted Ralston's personal check for $500 to start anew. Ralston, the banking genius, was quick to sympathize with the victim of a swindle, but he always nurtured a motive underneath his cloak of generosity. Sharon had revenge in his eyes and Ralston sensed, mistakenly, a future loyalty in the little man's desperation. Sharon would go to hell for him, if only to get even with the Comstock.

It was not typical banker's logic that dispatched William Sharon to Virginia City. Ralston had gambled on a gambler. Sharon soon paid off on his mentor's wager. He turned a fishy eye on the problems of depression, matter-of-factly donning a diver's suit to descend into the flooded bowels of the Gould and Curry. As Sharon waded through the murky sumps, he felt the strange pull and tug of the Big Magnet; he became a believer again. The Comstock, he was convinced, was not played out. He worked out a scheme to bring every last pickful of the fabled ore to the surface and into Ralston's vaults.

Ralston listened carefully to Sharon's plan. In order to avert complete disaster, the Bank must achieve total control over the Comstock Lode. Sharon offered to move to Virginia City and dedicate the next five years of his life to the project, if Ralston would establish a Comstock branch of the Bank of California under Sharon's stewardship. Ralston did not hesitate to bet the fortunes of his endangered banking empire on the daring strategy of William Sharon. The objections of the bank's conservative directors were swiftly overcome and, in September of 1864, Sharon opened for business at Taylor and C streets in Virginia City. The secret strategy of the Bank of California was nothing less than to buy up the entire Comstock Lode at depression prices.

In a last-ditch attempt to suck the water from the shafts so that mining could commence on the lower levels, Sharon ordered the Vulcan Iron Works to fabricate a new steam pump that would deliver 120 horsepower. Months would pass before the Vulcan pump was riveted into place on a gray concrete monolith in the sweating underground chambers of the Gould and Curry Mine. Ralston meanwhile was without the dividends to which he had become addicted, and the bank's reserves dried up like water in a drought.

Hedging his bets, Ralston turned finally to Adolph Sutro, the rugged genius who could see through mountains.

Sutro looked up from the ruins of his mill at the bottom of Six Mile Cañon and pondered his great tunnel to the heart of the Big Magnet. It must be built. But his personal fortune was meager. His stamp mill had recently burned, but even the insurance settlement could not finance his tunnel into the mountain of silver. "Crazy Sutro,"

WILLIAM SHARON

104

they called him. Crazy. He would show them. Adolph Sutro decided not to rebuild his mill. He would build his tunnel—no matter what it took. Somewhere he would find the money. He was to devote the next fifteen years of his life and a Scottish banker's fortune to this monumental task.

The Sutro Tunnel would run four miles from Carson River into the center of Sun Mountain. It would be the most ambitious engineering project ever attempted in America. The mines could be drained, revealing the huge capillaries of silver that snaked beneath the earth to depths below 1800 feet. The boys could breathe again, freed from the stench and reek and the long hours of brain-stabbing pain from the lack of oxygen. Death would no longer ride on the hissing vapors of phosphorated gases and the little wooden ore cars could rattle safely through his tunnel to mills that would be built along the Carson River.

Ralston delighted in the simple logic of Sutro's concept. He threw his support, but not his money, behind the Prussian immigrant's grand thoroughfare. It was Sutro's big chance, and he wasted no time. By March 1865, Sutro, on the strength of the banker's endorsement, had signed twenty-three of the major mining companies, representing 95 percent of the Comstock wealth, to contracts that guaranteed to pay the Tunnel company for drainage privileges a $2.00 royalty per ton of silver ore produced. Sutro agreed to match the owner's royalties with $3,000,000, which he had yet to raise from the tough and cautious Eastern venture capitalists who regarded the mutton-chopped promoter with studied skepticism from behind their mahogany desks. One of Ralston's provisos was that Sutro find other than western captial for the project. Ralston already had plans for all the money in the West. He armed Sutro with a letter of recommendation to the World Oriental Bank Corporation in London, a firm with which the Bank of California had done past business. Adolph Sutro departed the Comstock to attack the banking establishments of the East and of Europe, full of belief in his own destiny.

With Sutro abroad on his mission, Sharon was proceeding with his plan of monopoly. He began lending money at 5 percent, undercutting the competition's higher interest rates, until he put almost the entire Comstock in his debt. Then Sharon foreclosed without mercy. One by one the mills began to capitulate to what became known as Sharon's "Comstock Agency" and, if a mill balked at pressure from the Agency's suppliers, it was literally starved, cut off from capital and bank-controlled ore until it came to heel at Sharon's iron hand.

But still Sharon, for all his cold efficiency and cutthroat execution of his master plan, could not engineer a discovery. Without a new bonanza the Comstock was dead. Ralston came increasingly under the influence of his partner and figurehead president, Darius Ogden Mills. The conservative Mills, who listed himself in the San Francisco business directories simply as "D. O. Mills, Capitalist," had admonished Ralston to write off the Comstock so that he could look after his investments in California wine, textiles, agriculture, and shipping. "What right," said D. O. Mills, "has a bank gambling in mines?" But Sharon, poker player to the end, convinced Ralston that his empire was tied inexorably to the fortunes of the lode and that he had but one option. Sharon, as always, was thinking of himself first, and Ralston would have been well advised not to listen. The Bank of California, Sharon entreated, must take over operation of the Yellow Jacket and Chollar, two relatively water-free properties that Sharon now controlled, and uncover the next bonanza. Mills and the home-office directors were reluctant to take the risk, but knuckled under to Ralston when he pledged his personal fortune against possible losses. Not content with this exposure, Ralston signed a personal partnership agreement with Sharon and himself plunged head-on into twelve months' systematic exploration of the mines.

The venture was not the wild speculation that it appeared at first. In practical terms there was little water in the south end of the lode and the cost of deep exploration was easily recouped at a small profit from reworking old terrain. Meanwhile, Sharon sent down exaggerated reports of new discoveries, which bulled the stock market in San Francisco, allowing the bank crowd—as the San Francisco press called Ralston's consortium—to manipulate their holdings at the expense of other speculators, both big and small.

Late in the year 1865, after one false start, Sharon, from a 230-foot point of the Crown Point Mine, sank a "drift" into the adjoining Kentuck. A major ledge of silver was uncovered. Sharon had discovered a bonanza. The insiders' system went into effect, and Ralston began quietly purchasing all outstanding Kentuck stock. Ralston's big gamble had paid off and by December of 1865, Kentuck had coughed up a cool $2,000,000. Christmas was drunk and noisy at the San Francisco Stock Exchange on Pine Street. Ralston's dream of creating a Paris of the Pacific on San Francisco Bay seemed closer to reality.

Nearly everybody was getting rich now, or so it seemed. Even the quiet, lonely mining contractor, Irish John Mackay, had a piece of the Kentuck. Winter was washed down in a suds of champagne as the boys raised expensive hell in the saloons along C Street. Some of the most famous whores retired rich, and new belles from San Francisco's notorious Barbary Coast descended on Virginia City, riding in carriages like ladies of state.

During the spring and summer of '66, Adolph Sutro commuted in crowded railroad coaches between Boston, New York, and Washington, D.C., lobbying for government sanctions and contracts to raise his working capital of $3,000,000.

In New York he had published his first hard-sell propaganda "booklet" touting his tunnel as a key to the riches of the silver-hearted mountain. Powerful members of the eastern establishment, Vanderbilt, Astor, Morgan, and the great pathfinder John

Charles Frémont, were taken with the scope and grandeur of the fantastic four-mile underground corridor. But they found Sutro's plan suspect without the backing of the home bank in San Francisco. For what reason did Ralston, architect of the Comstock industrialization, say no? If Ralston would put up half a million to open the tunnel, they would subscribe three million from the east. Sutro put their proposition to Ralston. Instead of saying yes or no, Ralston kept saying maybe. An impatient Sutro persuaded the Nevada legislature to petition the federal Congress for financing.

With prospects of a congressional loan for Sutro's tunnel imminent, Ralston revealed the hand behind his stalling game. The bank's mines withdrew their proposed private subscription. Sharon wired Nevada's Senators Nye and Stewart, who withdrew congressional support; purses snapped shut all over California. The ongoing $2.00 royalty, if carried to extremes, could make Sutro a major financial power in the West; the man was too aggressive, too promotion-minded: he could be dangerous. More importantly, Sharon's new pumps were at last a match for the scalding floods. Ralston had changed his mind. In his grand scheme of things, he no longer needed the visionary engineer. Sutro was a genius, indeed a dangerous gregarious genius, a genius capable of romancing the eastern power elite. Ralston would not tolerate foreigners who might endanger the financial health of his still fragile San Francisco city state. The Bank of California's correspondent banks in Europe and New York broke off negotiations with Sutro. The Tunnel Company's credit became nonexistent. Even Sutro's friends nodded and hurriedly turned away from him on the streets. Sutro was suddenly locked out, blacklisted, a human liability on Ralston's balance sheet.

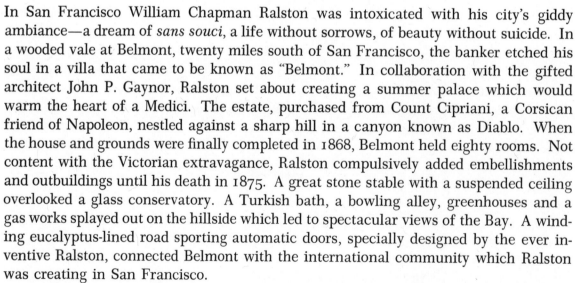

In San Francisco William Chapman Ralston was intoxicated with his city's giddy ambiance—a dream of *sans souci*, a life without sorrows, of beauty without suicide. In a wooded vale at Belmont, twenty miles south of San Francisco, the banker etched his soul in a villa that came to be known as "Belmont." In collaboration with the gifted architect John P. Gaynor, Ralston set about creating a summer palace which would warm the heart of a Medici. The estate, purchased from Count Cipriani, a Corsican friend of Napoleon, nestled against a sharp hill in a canyon known as Diablo. When the house and grounds were finally completed in 1868, Belmont held eighty rooms. Not content with the Victorian extravagance, Ralston compulsively added embellishments and outbuildings until his death in 1875. A great stone stable with a suspended ceiling overlooked a glass conservatory. A Turkish bath, a bowling alley, greenhouses and a gas works splayed out on the hillside which led to spectacular views of the Bay. A winding eucalyptus-lined road sporting automatic doors, specially designed by the ever inventive Ralston, connected Belmont with the international community which Ralston was creating in San Francisco.

The rich and powerful leading citizens of the day were transported in ever-growing numbers down the El Camino in Ralston's carriage-of-fours to Belmont, which became known as the White House of the Pacific. At the entrance of the palace, century-old oaks guarded magnolias and many-hued grass-held gardens, and red carnations cascaded over ancient Chinese urns like mysterious vermillion waterfalls. Inside the foyer classic columns stood reflected in the deep space of gigantic vertical mirrors, and crystal chandeliers floated from a four-story, etched glass skylight over the grand staircase.

In the drawing room business was discussed with visitors such as Secretary of State Anson Burlingame. Guests sat in solemn formation by orange-peel doors that moved slowly in a curved trace recalling the prows of steamboats. Then, as in the theater, a wall of etched glass rose slowly to reveal an immense banquet hall laden with the bounty of California. At each chair stood a robot like Chinese, a celestial in pigtail and silk. A clock etched into the center of a mirror announced midnight.

A gallery of white opera boxes rimmed with silver handrails looked down over a fantastic ballroom . . . and late into night after the traditional midnight suppers, William Chapman Ralston sat in the center box and watched the dancers float by in a golden glow of mirrors. The ambiance was of nineteenth-century Steamboat Gothic, no doubt influenced by Ralston's formative years on the Ohio and Mississippi rivers. But the style was more than monumental; it was a high drama of light, and it would echo on a grandiose scale in the court entrance of the Palace Hotel which the banker planned for San Francisco. The oval ballroom was surrounded by fourteen towering mirrors that caught every angle of light from the many amber, gaslit chandeliers, each with a different fixture. A dance floor patterned in alternating boards of maple and walnut, of light and dark, flowed like strange vertical currents under the black-tailed men and women wrapped in swirling dresses. But Ralston never danced. He watched it all in a mystical vision of light and motion until the tableau suspended into time, fading in an early morning reverie. Ralston often sat up all night this way.

The sandy-haired, portly banker with the massive, brooding face was a nervous dynamo. He could not stop. San Francisco must become a self-sufficient city state controlling the economy of the West. As a city-builder Ralston was without compeer. He filled in parts of the Bay and cut through hills and moved small mountains to make way for the saplings of commerce he planted in the city like a financial Johnny Appleseed. Mining equipment stood hot in the furnaces of his Vulcan Iron Works and silk for a textile industry rustled against redwood walls in his Visitacion Valley factory. He built shipyards and railroads, woolen mills, sugar refineries, and furniture factories. His cigar factory never came close to the pride of Havana, but his wineries equaled the best of Bordeaux. Comstock silver paid for all of this.

Toward the end of each working day Ralston's private coach left the French Renaissance Bank of California headquarters at California and Sansome streets and rolled across North Beach to the foot of Larkin Street, where the perspiring banker stripped and plunged into the bay for his constitutional swim halfway to Alcatraz Island and back. As Ralston's carriage returned, downtown workers stopped in the streets and tipped their hats to the Monte Cristo in their midst.

The fever of mining stock speculation in San Francisco surpassed even the combined frenzy of the Gold Rush of '49 and the Silver Rush of '59. People literally died from nervous exertion trying to make a killing in the market. By 1863 there were over 2000 mining corporations traded on the San Francisco Stock Exchange—that amounted to almost one company for every ten men in the city. Even with non-producing mines the stocks would soar, through competitive flights of fancy, to incredible highs. In the decade between 1865 and 1875 the paper value of Comstock stocks surpassed the amount of capital available on the entire Pacific Coast. When the crash came, as it inevitably would, the orgy of speculation would prove a greater financial disaster to San Francisco than the earthquake of 1906. But in the meantime, a few people got filthy rich. One of the filthiest was William Sharon.

The Iago of the Comstock Lode proved a master manipulator of the San Francisco stock market. Often, Sharon locked miners in the dark chambers of the Ophir on the pretext of keeping a new discovery secret when, in fact, there was only barren rock to report; Sharon's stocks would soar on the strength of such false rumors from Virginia City, which swept San Francisco's financial district saloons with tidal regularity, carrying the drinkers out into the street on a new wave of speculation. Sharon would even salt worthless rock with valuable ore to keep from the public the fact that a ledge was played out. Still, investors continued to dance like puppets to Sharon's strings.

In June 1867, the Union Mill and Mining Company was organized by a cabal of capitalists, who numbered among them Ralston, Mills, and Sharon. They thereby established the institution known as the "fortified monopoly system" on the Comstock. The power of the Union Mill was soon a fact of life in the mining community as its stockholders were revealed to be owners of the producing mines. The few independents such as Mackay and Fair, were hard-pressed to continue operations against the combine, which increased its holdings until it controlled seventeen mills and the majority of ore reduction in the district. Watersheds and timber of the Sierra Nevada and Lake Tahoe were then transformed into transportation and natural resource subsidiaries of the company, and the ancient redwood trees of the high Sierra fell to Sharon's axmen of avarice.

Financial success and unbridled capitalism had changed the rousing, good-natured vulgarity of the earlier-day Virginia City. People had become cynical, and in the saloons a bitter dialogue was heard. There was no point in fighting the company. It was merge or die on the Comstock. And men didn't trust each other anymore. But worst of all, the cosmic laughter of the boys didn't echo out of the saloons and whorehouses into the night streets, or if it did, the iron clank of round-the-clock industrialization soon drowned it out.

Still, a tough band of outsiders, holdouts against Sharon's combine, survived in the shadow of Sun Mountain. Taciturn John Mackay, after first becoming a tough and knowledgeable artisan, had set himself up as a contractor and had followed the custom of accepting a piece of the action for all or part of his construction work. The odds were long on this kind of barter, but soon Mackay held part ownership in four small mines and spoke of putting $25,000 away and getting out. A partnership with J. M. Walker in the Bullion Mine put an end to Mackay's hopes for early retirement when the Bullion failed. But Mackay refused to quit. He stubbornly continued to trade sweat equity for a few feet in any new claim, because he knew that between the big producing mines lay unclaimed slices which might one day open up into a large vein—if only they could dig deep enough. Mackay's lucky shot came when, with Walker, he finally managed to trade for control of the little-regarded Kentuck mine that lay beside the Crown Point in Gold Hill. The Kentuck had produced only low-grade ore and nobody thought much of it, but the gamble paid off when a rich vein was uncovered below layers of worthless rock.

After John Mackay had finally amassed a sizable nest egg from his investment in the Kentuck Mine, he did not retire as was his announced intention. Instead he married the widowed daughter of Colonel Hungerford, veteran of the Piute war, and built a home for his new family above C Street. His neighbor was James G. Fair, the crafty superintendent of the Ophir. Fair's experience as a successful mining operator in California, coupled with his knowledge and utilization of advanced mining technology, had made him a new figure to be reckoned with in Virginia City. He and Mackay had not given up hope of finding the great vein which both men were certain lay hidden somewhere below the deepest shafts of the Ophir and Gould and Curry mines.

By 1867 Mackay had risen to the position of superintendent of the Kentuck Mine. Publicly he occupied a position of limited power in the employ of Sharon's puppet directors. Privately he had quietly begun to invest his personal funds in exploration and development of the elusive big strike. Mackay and Fair, with the encouragement of their friends Flood and O'Brien, proprietors of the Auction Lunch Saloon in San Francisco, resolved to stand together on the Comstock, there to pursue a defensive, yet independent, strategy that would nullify Sharon's checkmate.

The Fourth of July found Adolph Sutro in Washington, D.C., fighting time and the Bank of California. Sutro was not a man to be put down by a banker, even a banker

Overleaf:
RUMORS FROM VIRGINIA CITY HIT SAN FRANCISCO

with the power of William Chapman Ralston. He took an oath to expose the bank crowd's combine on the Comstock for the vicious monopoly that it was. Sutro planned to make his tunnel a political cause, to turn the people against the arrogant bonanza tyrants, Ralston and Sharon. He would go into the mines, to the boys who hacked away at the earth in the catacombs beneath C Street and gain their support. Sutro set about to forge a unique axis, a coalition between the working miners and the czars of eastern finance, a concept combining his empathy for the people with his drive for power. Always a man who reveled in the drama of a situation that involved a heroic concept, Sutro resorted to inflammatory pamphleteering. A man ahead of his time, he used the most advanced technology of propaganda—even unto magic lantern shows. He printed posters. He wrote "canned" editorials supporting his cause and sent them to newspapers that invariably printed them. He rattled the gates of the Congress of the United States, and he waved the endorsement of Nevada's legislature before any politician he could find. But Congress would not convene until December, so Sutro, already low on funds, embarked on a whirlwind tour of European capitals, where he obtained testimonials from John Stuart Mills, the worldly philosopher, Bernhard von Cotta, the geologist, Julius Weisbach, the engineer, and other scientific experts of the day. But learned testimonials did not sway the foreign bankers. The unsuccessful Sutro returned to New York to find himself the butt of ridicule, and masterful ridicule at that. Wrote Mark Twain:

> Mr. A. Sutro of the great Sutro Tunnel scheme arrived yesterday from Europe on the *Russia*. He brought his tunnel back with him. He failed to sell it to the Europeans. They said it was a good tunnel, but that they would look around a little before purchasing; if they could not find a tunnel to suit them nearer home they would call again. Many capitalists were fascinated with the idea of owning a tunnel, but none wanted such a long tunnel, or one that was so far away that they could not walk out afternoons and enjoy it.

Sutro returned to Washington broke. Only the sale of a $200 lot in California saw him through the winter in the capital. It was, however, to be a life-giving transaction. At the eleventh hour, the Congressional Committee on Mines and Mining recommended a $5,000,000 loan secured by a government mortgage on Sutro's Nevada properties. Ralston was furious. Urgent messages from Sharon and the principal mine superintendents, including Mackay, who also feared Sutro, were wired to Senators Nye and Stewart in Washington, and vicious editorials appeared in powerful dailies of the times. The fine hand of Ralston could be seen between the lines of type. To add insult to injury, Sutro was accused of bribing Congress.

Summoning up his political genius and penchant for showmanship, Sutro loosed a barrage of propaganda upon the Congress of the United States. Testimonials, pamphlets, and letters of endorsement swirled into a cyclone of publicity until Sutro's tunnel was a cause célèbre in Washington. Then, Thaddeus Stevens of Pennsylvania—champion of a repressive Reconstruction policy—spoke out in behalf of the tunnel; Adolph Sutro had found his long-sought champion at last. The old and great political patriarch, the powerful elder statesman of the Republican Party, would lead the fight from the floor of the Senate. The Senate was busy impeaching Lincoln's successor, Andrew Johnson, and those hearings would buy time to fight Ralston's smear campaign. As Sutro made ready for a triumphal visit home, he received terrible news. Stevens was dead.

Ralston had won again, and his megalomaniacal devotion to San Francisco became insatiable. Nothing was too big or too good for his city. As he raced along El Camino Real to San Francisco in his carriage like a Caesar, his loyal mechanics, under Sharon, were pressing every last drop of silver from the deep-struck ore of the Comstock. Yet, major producers were petering out and the accursed Sutro and his tunnel were still a menace. He must go deeper into the mines. Sharon must deliver another bonanza, a new conquest.

Eager to please his mentor, Sharon soon brought forth one more moneymaking idea, one that had been kicked around the Comstock before. His mines were on the wane and the mills were running out of worthwhile ore, so he needed this new venture as much as Ralston. As usual, it would bring new revenues to the coffers of the Bank of California.

A railroad was Sharon's answer, a railroad that would complete his Comstock monopoly. By January of 1869, under Sharon's superintendent, Hume Yerrington, work was begun on a winding twenty-one-mile monstrosity of rails that ran from the Carson River up the mountain through Silver City and then up to D Street in Virginia.

Sharon masterfully finagled the Nevada counties of Ormsby, Lyon, and Storey into donating almost $500,000 as a gift for the "common good." Then, by forcing the mining companies to shift commitments originally made to the Sutro Tunnel Company to his Virginia and Truckee Railroad, he raised the remaining $700,000 of the construction costs. Immediately, three steam engines were begun by bank-controlled manufacturers in San Francisco. Donor-counties in Nevada were rewarded by inscribing their names in gold on Ralston's "iron horses." Labor was provided by some 1500 Chinese coolies, who toiled like ants for a mere fraction of the going $4.00-a-day wage paid the Miners' Union members. And Adolph Sutro, now back in the Comstock without his

Overleaf:
THE VIRGINIA AND TRUCKEE RAILROAD

congressional loan, watched with righteous rage as the Chinese laid down the track like huge iron chopsticks over the rocky surface of the mountains.

With the completion of the Virginia and Truckee Railroad, one main purpose of the tunnel as a direct link from the Carson River to the mines was defeated. The bank now controlled nearly all phases of Comstock mining. Sutro, in desperation, turned all his energies to convincing the miners of the dangers in the deep shafts. He predicted underground fires. Only his tunnel would make them safe. The boys listened—and then went on digging. They were not interested in expensive life insurance.

By the New Year of 1869, Ralston had overextended himself. His San Francisco real estate ventures were faltering. His textile and agricultural industries were damaged by floods and fire and could not support themselves, and he was in debt to support his monthly dividend to stockholders. He looked again to the Comstock for help, and found instead that his mines were petering out. To add to his grief, the Miners' Union was raising hell over wages on the Comstock and Ralston was being forced to make promises he couldn't keep.

In the midst of this travail came a new challenge from the East. The Union Pacific and Southern Pacific Railroads, joined together by a final spike driven at Promontory, Utah, brought goods and commodities competition to California. It was the beginning of the end of Ralston's economic hammerlock on the western economy.

Meanwhile, Ralston was ignorant of a palace coup in the making. Mackay, superintendent of the Kentuck, and Fair, of the Ophir, were sure of a new bonanza discovery. With inside information about trouble at court and their expert knowledge of diminishing productivity of the mines, the acquisitive Irishmen bid for control of the Hale and Norcross Mine.

When Sharon "locked" two-dozen miners at the 900-foot level of the Hale and Norcross to prevent them from "leaking" news of a "secret" bonanza to the rumor-infested San Francisco Exchange, the Irishmen recognized it as an old trick to raise the price of bank crowd stock.

After a brief flurry, which benefited the bankers, the staged "discovery" did not pan out and stock in the Hale and Norcross fell to $11.00 per share. Then Sharon woke to shocking news. The Irishmen, with backing from Messrs. Flood and O'Brien, had bought half the shares in the Hale and Norcross Mine at the cheap prices.

Acting on a tip from Mackay, Flood beat Ralston to the remaining stock by twelve scant hours. Control had passed to Mackay, Fair, Flood, and O'Brien on the sale of stock by an unsuspecting San Francisco widow.

The Irishmen consolidated their victory by installing Jim Fair as superintendent of the Hale and Norcross Mine. With improved equipment and technical skills, reflecting years of struggle in the underground chambers of the Comstock, they gradually developed new ore and replaced stockholder assessments with a dividened from quad-rupled earnings. Within months the Irishmen had opened their own mill to process Hale and Norcross ore—a new threat to the Union Mill and Mining combine.

Only one Comstock mine, other than the pride of the Irishmen, showed any promise. On April 7, 1869, Ralston opened an emergency telegram with trembling hands. It was not the bonanza news that he had been waiting for.

The Yellow Jacket Mine in Gold Hill, which contained his one remaining vein of promise, was on fire. Flames cut off the 1000-foot main chamber and many miners had roasted to death. An elevator exploded to the surface, carrying suffocating miners who told of the horror below. Other twisted metal cages shot up carrying a hideous cargo of maimed and decapitated bodies. The stench of burning flesh filled the throats of comrades and relatives who waited at the opening of the shaft.

A lantern, lowered with emergency instructions, returned without a telltale tug of life; and once Superintendent John P. Jones had entered the shaft to shut off the blowers fanning the flames with oxygen, the rescue mission became a death watch. Forty-five men perished in the chain reaction of fire and explosions that raged for months. Later, at the end of summer, the charred and decomposed remains of Washoe's finest were lifted silently to the surface.

The Big Magnet at last had its revenge on William Chapman Ralston. In San Fran-cisco the market was a scene of wholesale panic as rumors of arson whistled up Mont-gomery Street. Ralston personally donated relief money to the families of the victims of the Yellow Jacket Fire. But his alms for the dead were accepted with anger rather than gratitude.

This was Adolph Sutro's moment of destiny. He rose to the occasion with a theatri-cality that was to anticipate the uses of media in American politics. He saturated the mines and the entire Comstock with wild, inflammatory posters for a scheduled mass meeting with the mineworkers in Virginia City. His propaganda excelled. The boys hung from every wall and balcony at Maguire's (later Piper's) Opera House on D Street, and they heard his heavily accented German baritone lay bare the shocking facts of Ralston's disintegrating Comstock empire. The bank had foreclosed on innocent vic-tims of its own conspiracies. The bank had imported cheap coolie labor. And the bank had sabotaged the Sutro Tunnel, caring nothing for the lives of the miners who brought the riches of the Big Magnet to daylight!

Sutro's sweating audience erupted into a paroxysm of shouting anger. Sharon would have been lynched from the balcony of the International Hotel that night had not Sutro

Overleaf:
THE YELLOW JACKET MINE DISASTER

calmed the boys with his plan of action. In a capitalistic peoples' revolt, the muckers each plunked down ten bucks per month to finance the Sutro Tunnel Company's four-mile enterprise. The boys admired a man who took on giants.

On August 25, 1869, the Miners' Union of Virginia City and Gold Hill adopted the following resolution:

> RESOLVED, by the miners of the Virginia and Gold Hill Unions, in joint convention assembled, that, as an earnest of our faith in the results to spring from the construction of the Sutro Tunnel, as a great rational work, and a financial operation, we do hereby agree to subscribe to the stock of the Sutro Tunnel Co., the sum of $50,000 in United States gold coin, as a first installment, payable immediately and for the purpose of starting work upon the tunnel itself without delay.

On October 19, 1869, Sutro opened the mouth of his tunnel. At the rate of 160 feet a month, he burrowed and hacked his way toward the heart of the Big Magnet. He had a long four miles to go.

Ralston and Sharon now faced a hostile and potentially powerful coalition on the Comstock. But the hated Sutro, the holdout Irishmen, and the union laborers were not without their own troubles. Mackay and Fair had pumped much of their Hale and Norcross money back into a failing Bullion and Savage Mine. It was an expensive lesson in deep-level mining, and their saloonkeeper partners—turned brokers—were worried. Sutro cautioned them to wait until he could drain off the underground floors, but the Irishmen stubbornly continued to explore the lower levels. John Mackay was convinced that a great strike, the greatest of all bonanzas, lay in a thin ledge, 1310 feet between the Ophir and the Gould and Curry, both faded stars of the Ralston galaxy. Certain experts, like mining editor Dan De Quille of the *Enterprise*, agreed with them, and in 1869 Ralston, not one to leave any stone unturned, had founded the Virginia Consolidated Mining Company to protect and explore this deeper ledge. The "Con Virginia," as it was to become known in the financial capitals of the world, incorporated little-known and small mines with names like "Dick Sides," "White and Murphy," and "Kinney." But it had been plagued by repeated flooding. Finally, a discouraged Ralston dumped the stock on the San Francisco market. Flood and O'Brien, at the insistence of their Virginia City partners bought a controlling interest in the Consolidated Virginia for as low as fifteen cents a share. Ralston, the great financial genius, the visionary doge of Belmont, had sold out the supermine of the Comstock. The Con Virginia, pride of the holdout Irishmen, was soon to become the greatest of all bonanzas.

Sutro was a monster of purpose oblivious to the machinations of his enemies as he burrowed into the mountain. Meanwhile, in Washington, Ralston's agents introduced a congressional bill to repeal his tunnel rights. The bank crowd envied Sutro his popularity and influence with the miners and lawmakers, and they coveted his $2.00 royalty, but what they truly feared was that Sutro in his pestiferous tunneling would discover the big bonanza.

Sutro raced east to defend himself. He collared Congressman Blair of the Ways and Means Committee, an ardent Sutro backer. Blair delivered an impassioned speech to Congress eloquently describing the Yellow Jacket Fire and condemning the Bank's expansionist activities.

On Saint Patrick's Day, 1870, the Congress voted 124 to 42 against repeal. Sutro was becoming a master politician on Capitol Hill.

Ralston had failed in his sabotage, and he had yet another setback coming. With Sharon's encouragement, he had authorized development of the Crown Point Mine, installing John P. Jones, the burly Welsh hero of the Yellow Jacket Fire, as superintendent. Jones worked from the 1100-foot level in crosscut section and found nothing; and when at last Ralston began to lose faith, Jones prevailed on his immediate superior, Director Alvinza Hayward, to purchase large quantities of the depressed Crown Point stock. Soon Hayward and Jones had secretly controlled the mine, and a small but rich vein of silver was slowly being uncovered in a fissure below Gold Hill. Ralston, who had been a friend and backer of both Hayward and Jones, was deeply offended by what he considered their personal disloyalty. As the news of the discovery leaked out he decided to retaliate. Sharon thought the find was not important, and he tried to gull Hayward and Jones by selling a large block of stock at a high price. To the great surprise of even the most seasoned speculators, Hayward bought all of Sharon's stock for almost a million and a half dollars. Then, while Sharon bragged of his sucker sale, Jones brought in a $3,000,000 bonanza.

Sharon was furious, and Ralston felt deeply a Judas in his midst. But the hurt was short-lived. The Belcher Mine, a Ralston property adjoining Crown Point, opened into a wider vein. It was as if a great x-ray of a human hand filled with a thousand silver capillaries had emerged from the earth. The vein discovered in the Belcher was an extension of Hayward's and Jones's ledge and delivered an even larger bonanza—the largest yet. The worth of the Belcher exceeded that of Crown Point by $5,000,000. Ralston had been saved by the Comstock once more.

Ralston, like all geniuses, was a study in excess and contradiction. He was content to plunder the Comstock through the cruelest exercises of monopoly, for the Big Magnet was a means to an end, the lavishing of love on his home city. On the Comstock he was an absentee tyrant. At home, he was benevolent, helping his friends, backing men with new ideas, nurturing the arts, helping the poor, and entertaining visitors in high style at Belmont.

The bold and intricate tapestry that was Ralston's monopoly had begun to shred. But

Ralston seemed not to care. As he sat in his silver-rimmed box in Belmont, as the dancers whirled below him against the strange, striped, parquet floor, Ralston's late-night reveries gave up a larger inspiration. He was building a great hotel in San Francisco. Nothing mattered now but the Palace Hotel. This opulent hostelry rising out of the grassy sand dunes off Market Street must be a jewel of the Americas, a glistening, colonnaded structure lighted with etched glass and embellished with California laurelwood and gold. Again, in collaboration with architect Gaynor, Ralston became totally immersed in a drama of enclosed space.

Exterior marble walls held low-arched classic columns, and within the theme of the rotunda gallery at Belmont was rendered on a monumental scale. The interior court entrance of Ralston's Palace was the dénouement of a rich and theatrical use of architecture. The lofty, pillared court rose for seven stories over colonnaded balconies to enclose a space larger than the greatest underground gallery of the Comstock Lode.

The ground floor was cut into a circular driveway, paved with marble, and overhead, an arched roof of glass illuminated the towering pagan façade of the interior court. Beyond the carriage entrance, black and white marble floors held palms concealed by carved screens. Against the colonnades tropical plants nestled against sweet-smelling orange and lime trees that ripened in the late afternoon over an ambiance of Gypsy violins.

Each floor gave up homage to the California economy, and on every level a liveried attendant maintained an annunciator and pneumatic tubes for immediate communication with the main office. All linens and silver, all imported china were monogrammed, and in the dazzling kitchen an army of chefs presided over preparations for a dining saloon that seated 1200 persons.

Above the grand ballroom, a second floor held committee rooms where high stakes cards were drawn and where one could entertain a lady in the privacy of seven small dining rooms. Every mantel held a timepiece from Ralston's Cornell Watch Factory, each stick of furniture was cut from California laurel at the "West Coast Furniture Factory," and all appointments were forged or spun or polished by Ralston's workers. Under the marble floor four artesian wells fed 28,000 gallons of water per hour to the hotel. The Palace had 700 rooms and 9000 spitoons. The carpets were imported from France. The elevators were elegantly mirrored. It was the biggest hotel in America.

Nothing was too elegant or too grandiose for San Francisco. The Palace was four times too big for the city. It would cost millions.

Ralston stepped up his feverish pace. The elaborate late-night entertainments continued, and as he raced back and forth between Belmont and the city his face bore a florid look, and, beneath the elegant cut of his clothes, his body bulged in proportions that were more than Victorian.

Friends noticed that he tore nervously at pads of paper while talking and that his eyes reflected a curious nostalgia.

For all Ralston's glory he remained sensitive to fame and never lost the common touch. Personally, he was a kind and generous man, and, for an empire builder, bashful. When the directors of the Central Pacific Railroad proposed honoring Ralston by naming a California agricultural community in the San Joaquin Valley after the state's most important and revered citizen, Ralston demurred. He rose and declined the honor in a terse attack on self-aggrandizement, and as he sat down, a friend observed that Ralston was indeed a modest man. A standing ovation followed. The Spanish word for modest, "*Modesto,*" was put before the convention, and the dusty railroad town grew to prosper as Modesto, California.

But many people hated Ralston. He was, to them, the smiling mandarin behind the vicious and coldhearted Sharon.

The Franco-Prussian War had put an end to Sutro's hope of a loan from friendly Paris bankers, and he was once again back in Washington fighting Ralston's agents. To prove to the lawmakers that he was telling the truth about the future of the tunnel, Sutro pushed President Ulysses S. Grant to send a congressional commission to the Comstock. And in the summer of June 1871, two West Point generals, a group of army engineers, and a professor of geology arrived to inspect the mines.

The commissioners found a fantastic 200-mile maze of underground catacombs, the product of some twelve years of mining operation. But the unsuspecting contingent from the Hudson was deceived by Sharon's superintendents. Never did the West Point men see the inside of the collapsed and flooded chambers nor breathe the foul burning air of the deepest shafts. And when they inspected Sutro's tunnel, Sharon's toadies prejudiced them at every turn with false information.

In the midst of this planned obstruction, representatives of the London banking house of McCalmont arrived on the Comstock and sought out Sutro. The Scotsmen had no association with the bank of California and wanted none. The bankers, impressed by the Belcher and Crown Point's continuing bonanzas, returned to the British Isles, and to Sutro's great surprise, they soon invited him to England, where they opened their purses to the tune of $650,000. The canny McCalmonts knew a sure thing when they saw it, and there was no doubt in their minds that a wider vein lay beneath the existing bonanza.

Buoyed by the Scottish bankers' support, Sutro expanded his activities. He named his company site after himself, and a model town grew around the opening in the mountain. Churches, hotels, dance halls, saloons, ironworks, and a newspaper were added to the new town of Sutro, where the residential streets were named after women—Adele through Jeanne—predating the contemporary system of naming hurricanes. Four hundred workers went into the tunnel day and night. By the end of 1871, Sutro had bored over a half mile into the Big Magnet.

While Sutro was burrowing and blasting, the army engineers returned to their fortress on the Hudson and dictated their report to Congress. The report was full of misrepresentations, and on every page Sutro read the heavy hand of Sharon. Sutro was beside himself with rage. Sharon's sharp young mining superintendents had hoodwinked the generals. The report could force the Scottish bankers to withdraw.

Sutro filed a formal complaint with the Committee of Mines and Mining in Washington. In the capital he buttonholed the Secretary of War, who ordered the West Point commission to report to Washington on the double. Then as the recalled commissioners sat before the committee, Sutro, the prosecutor from Sun Mountain, interrogated them for twenty-four days like a professional trial lawyer. Ralston sent the bank's wiliest attorney to Washington. Claiming slander, mine superintendents Day, Batterman, and Regun soon followed. It was a grand and classic battle. Adolph Sutro, his own lawyer, mining engineer, metallurgist, geologist, and more importantly, his own man, faced the hired liars of William Chapman Ralston.

In the congressional hearing, using a magic lantern show as a visual aid, Sutro demonstrated his superior intellectual energy and his firsthand knowledge of European mining techniques and physics. His rapid-fire calculations gave a convincing air of authority. Ralston's captains of industry formed a strident and depressing counterpoint to Sutro's lone voice of humanity. This image of one man standing up to the corrupt obstructionists of progress won the Committee to his cause.

Congress received a bill recommending an additional $2,000,000 mortgage on Sutro's land and equipment, and the Scottish bankers extended an additional $800,000 line of credit. Mark Twain revised his opinion of the man whose tunnel had been so widely considered folly: "Mr. Sutro, the originator of this prodigious enterprise, is one of the few men in the world who is gifted with the pluck and perseverance necessary to follow up and hound such an undertaking to completion."

Ralston took his defeat with a grain of ennui. His many enterprises were consuming his energy. He had shipped Comstock bullion overseas to mint the first Japanese yen, and the completion of the Palace Hotel had become his magnificent obsession, a relief from the toil and struggle of empire-building. After banker's hours, he often stood alone in the soft light of the glass-domed Palace courtyard. For it was in the architectural extravagance of the Palace Hotel that Ralston's dreams were realized in never-changing rose-glow, where life was always three o'clock in the afternoon and he could forget about the Big Magnet.

Sharon had evened his score with the Comstock and had retired to San Francisco, where he managed his interests with Ralston. It was decided to send him to Washington as a senator from Nevada to oppose Sutro's tunnel in caucus and cloakroom. It was a foregone conclusion that the rich little man would be elected.

However, it wasn't a foregone conclusion to John P. Jones, the Welsh superintendent turned mining titan. He billed himself as the "Great Commoner," and with the aid of

Joe Goodman of the *Territorial Enterprise* he campaigned against William Sharon. The vengeful Sharon publicly accused Jones of setting the torch to the Yellow Jacket Mine. He had gone too far, even for politics of his day. The charge of arson backfired. Jones challenged Sharon to a duel—which was declined—and in Virginia City the *Enterprise* exposed Sharon's attempted $50,000 bribe of one Isaac Hubbel, underground foreman at Crown Point, as a witness to arson. No one would believe that Jones, hero of the Yellow Jacket disaster, would set a fire that would kill his own men. Hubbel had borne false witness and Sharon was investigated by the Storey County grand jury for bribery. Ralston was angered by his partner's gross behavior, and when the jury exonerated Jones and Sharon bitterly withdrew his candidacy, word around the saloons was that the banker had a hand in the decision. Jones went to the Senate.

In March of 1873 strange things were happening in the candlelit darkness at the 1167-foot level of the Con Virginia. Fair had found something. A razor-thin blue black shard appeared slicing through the Gould and Curry, to the Belcher, and finally cracking sharply down into the lowest levels of Con Virginia and the neighboring little California mine. It led to the heart of the Big Magnet. Fair and Mackay told only their two countrymen. Each day in San Francisco, Flood and O'Brien quietly purchased all the remaining cheap stock in the Con Virginia and the California mines. Down the street at California and Sansome, Sharon scoffed at "those Irishmen" and Ralston fought with his directors over the outlandish cost of the Palace Hotel.

From the saloons along C Street in Virginia City came the sounds of grumbling.

Slippery Jim Fair was hiring a hand-picked crew of deep-level miners. No drunks or smokers need apply, and, according to scuttlebutt, only clean-cut young men or trusted veterans had seen the deep cloistered chambers of the Con Virginia and they weren't talking. Their lips had been sealed by bonus stock.

By the late fall of 1873, Mackay and Fair controlled the little wedge that the bankers had orphaned.

Their 1310 feet lay innocently between the Gould and Curry and Ophir Mines, the north 600 incorporated into the California Mining Company, the south 700 dealt off to the Consolidated Virginia. Now, with the consummate hype of master poker players, Mackay and Fair made their move. Dan De Quille was invited down to have a look.

De Quille stepped from the elevator cage onto the biggest bonanza in modern times. The main chamber was cut into a floor that widened from 30 to 54 feet extending along a 140-foot corridor of solid silver. Overhead, walls rose into a 20-foot ceiling. De Quille was stunned. He was confronted with a room whose walls and floors and ceilings assayed to $632 per ton.

The mining editor poked about the iridescent black chamber in the heart of the Big Magnet. At the far end of the corridor, great luminous shadows played like manganese blue fingers on the green-spotted surface of the monumental altar of rock. De Quille slowly paced off the perimeters of the ledge, and then in a measured silent ritual, he appraised the treasure. Three million dollars a month for a year would flow to the Irishmen from the underground draft in the California and Con Virginia mines.

Other experts confirmed the unbelievable estimate of a bonanza worth $230,000,000 —at a minimum. Deidesheimer, the inventor of square-set timbering, personally surveyed the Con Virginia and, with overstatement untypically German, blurted out a figure of $1.5 billion. The Con Virginia stock responded in heights more familiar to astronomy than finance. It went from $90 to $790 a share. Police had to cordon off the crowds trying to get into the Stock Exchange to buy.

The Irishmen were the new kings of the Comstock. Between the 1200- and 1500-foot levels, their crisscrossed drifts and shafts held a solid formation of the richest silver ore imaginable. The sheered-off expanse of black and gray rock formed a fantastic bas-relief deep in the earth. The walls, floors, and ceilings of this angled, wood-framed underground pyramid were incrusted with a composition of green-spotted gold and translucent quartz that reflected smoky light from the miners' lamps like prisms.

Ralston's position was in jeopardy, and the banking titans scurried in ever-decreasing circles around the perimeter of their empire. Only Sharon rested comfortably on his hoarded profits. Adolph Sutro continued to bore into the mountain as the outside world was electrified by the discovery of the biggest bonanza ever. In Europe, Bismarck reformed his silver-standard monetary system and the House of Rothschild speculated heavily in Comstock securities. Congress watched the rich western mountain with increasing vigilance.

By 1874, Virginia City, reflecting the treasure chest underneath it, was the richest town of its size in the world. To the delight of an increasingly cosmopolitan populace, the sumptuous daily bill of fare at the International Hotel on C Street included champagne, caviar, truffles, oysters, and lobster shipped from the Atlantic Coast on ice. Forty thousand people lived in Storey County, and the state of Nevada literally manufactured its own money. A century later the silver dollars that rolled out of the Carson Mint would become collector's items worth thirty times the paper "fiat" dollar issued by the U.S. Treasury.

Below Virginia, the town of Sutro had grown to a population of nearly 1000 souls, 400 of whom toiled around the clock in the 140-degree heat of the tunnel. The battle of the titans became a race between the Irish, digging downward, and Sutro, tunneling inward, to see who would first reach the core of the mountain. The underground contest took on attributes of a sporting event, but both sides were in deadly earnest. When Sutro completed his tunnel he would control Sun Mountain. The proud Irish quartet worked their men overtime to take out as many tons of ore as possible before they would have to pay Sutro an ounce of tribute. Sutro's men bored and blasted into the hard Washoe rock at a rate that often slowed to fifty feet per month. Then swelling white blobs of clay oozed between the cracks that formed around the diamond drill heads. The miners' tools stuck like toothpicks in the thick white bubble gum that hardened in the surrounding deoxygenized air, and men and mules alike fainted in the rutted tracks along the corridors. Sutro stripped to the waist and took his shift with his men, swearing in German as he hacked at the retreating "header" wall.

The heat rose to an unbearable 170 degrees, and there was not enough oxygen to fan the smallest flame. Candles could not burn, yet Sutro and his men heroically worked on in the stinking darkness. The atmosphere became hallucinatory, and it was no longer possible to smell the rotten sulfurous air. Sutro's "folly" was Dante's hell. Finally, giant 900-foot air shafts were sunk at maximum intervals into the roof of the tunnel, and blowers and compressors gave momentary relief to workers who now donned ice helmets to stay alive. At the entrance of the tunnel, the men doused their bodies with melting, brownish chunks of ice from Sutro's ice factory.

In the saloons the muckers marveled mockingly at Sutro's powder monkeys as they staggered out of their hole in the base of the mountain. They laughed into the night at the stories of mules' noses stuck in air holes and they debated the relative intelligence of the stubborn little beasts when their "monkey" masters had to pull them away from the oxygen with winches.

The Irish Bonanza Kings, who were no less autocratic than their predecessors, soon allied with the bank crowd against Sutro; they too saw the tunnel with its $2.00 royalty as a threat to their new-found supremacy on the Comstock—a supremacy in which they were to surpass their Protestant banker rivals in the uses and abuses of monopoly. Sutro's trusted engineer and best friend was killed in an explosion that had all the tell-tale marks of sabotage. Still Sutro pressed on.

Ralston was convinced that the Irishmen's bonanza extended into the Ophir. But when he staged a desperate last rally to save his Comstock empire, Sharon, ever Brutus to Ralston's Caesar, stabbed him in the back. As Ralston bulled the Ophir stock to outrageous levels on the San Francisco Exchange, Sharon declared for the Senate again. He financed his 1874 campaign to succeed Nevada's retiring senator, Bill Stewart, by short-selling Ophir stock in a way that finished Ralston on the Comstock.

The United States Senate was at that time a millionaire's club where seats were bought and paid for. Senators more often represented business "constituencies" than the masses, but so blatant and venal were Sharon's two attempts to buy his place in electoral history that the little man was in large measure responsible for Nevada's lasting reputation as a "rotten borough" where absentee millionaires bought themselves six-year, duty-free vacations in Washington, D.C. In his second and successful grab for the Senate brass ring, Sharon purchased for cash the soul of his most strident critic, the *Territorial Enterprise*. The *Enterprise* had consistently referred to Sharon as a "hyena," among less kind epithets, but under its new management the Quaker politician was described in terms normally reserved for the second coming of Christ.

Sharon secured his U.S. Senate seat by bribing the entire Nevada state legislature, a body accustomed to the palms-outstretched position. Then with Ophir stock at a near-record high and going higher, he sold his large holdings short. At the same time a rumor, traced by many to Sharon, swept Montgomery Street that the Ophir was in borrasca. Ophir stock crashed like a gargoyle in an earthquake and Sharon made an unconscionable profit on his short-selling. The senator-elect had the cheek to buy back Ophir shares at bargain prices from many of the friends and political supporters he had sold out. Among those crushed in the Ophir crash was his partner, William Chapman Ralston.

Without the infusion of capital from the Ophir that he had counted on, Ralston was gasping for money, a poor fish out of water. The eastern financial panic of 1873 that started with the failure of Jay Cooke's New York banking empire was just being felt on the West Coast in the summer of 1875. The money market was as tight as an air lock, and a rival San Francisco bank founded by the Bonanza Kings—the Bank of Nevada—began to further tighten the screws on the beleaguered Bank of California. The bank was frightfully overextended; not the least of its unsecured problems was a $4.5 million overdraft in Ralston's personal account. The banker's last great, expensive hope—a takeover of San Francisco's Spring Valley Water Company—was stalled by political maneuvering. He found himself adrift in a sea of hostility. The venomous, sensational attacks on Ralston by the San Francisco *Call* and the *Bulletin* were at last taking their toll, at home and abroad. When the Oriental Bank of London refused to extend Ralston's credit, businessmen began to shuffle past the ornate bronze doors of his bank with anxiety written on the blank checks of their faces.

On August 26, 1875, the one great fear of bankers materialized. The widow, the shopkeeper, the merchant, and the big depositor were all seized with the same emotion at the same time. Panic hit the bank, and screaming, frightened depositors pushed from Montgomery Street to California and Sansome to close out their accounts. The bank bled gold that day, and when the great doors clanked shut, Ralston sat among the overdrafts of his empire.

The next afternoon the great man waited outside the board room in a deserted Bank of California while his friends decided his fate. It was not long in coming. Senator Sharon immediately called for Ralston's ouster. The directors, for whom he had made millions, sat cowardly behind closed doors while Ralston signed the resignation Darius Ogden Mills placed before him. The meeting was adjourned. Ralston was ruined. At four o'clock, leaving his valuables in the charge of the custodian at the Neptune Beach House, he went for his customary swim in San Francisco Bay.

No one could say for sure what happened that day near Alcatraz Island, but just before sunset, the lifeless body of William Chapman Ralston was hauled from the gray water at the foot of Leavenworth Hill. Ralston's friends said that the always hypertensive banker had suffered a stroke. But his enemies, among whom must be numbered the offensive Sharon, put the word about that he was a suicide. The vengeful *Bulletin* went so far as to print a baseless rumor that Ralston had swallowed a vial of poison before plunging into the bay. San Franciscans turned out in a three-mile funeral procession and gave the banker a hero's farewell. He was forty-nine.

Gertrude Atherton, the novelist and first lady of California letters, knew Ralston as a young girl. She dismisses all talk of the banker's suicide in her intimate history of California, quoting a private letter written to one of Ralston's daughters by his doctor, John Pitman—the last man to see the great man alive—as the final word on what really happened that afternoon:

FORT WAYNE, INDIANA, *January 5, 1903.*

DEAR MADAM,—I have to-day received a letter from Mr. Charles E. Dark, of Indianapolis, telling me of your serious desire to have a statement from me regarding the death of your father, Mr. W. C. Ralston, whom it was my pleasure and honor to know.

If I remember correctly it was August, 1875. He was President of the California Woolen Mills, California Furniture Company, and the Bank of California. He had for some time been almost pursued by Senator Sharon, whose manipulations caused the suspension of the Bank of California, which was totally unnecessary, as the bank was solvent; but Sharon played his cards causing the suspension. The day of Mr. Ralston's death was a blazing hot day, the city was a furnace of heat. I met him as he was coming out of the bank and shook hands with him. He told me he had just shifted a load of care from his shoulders by resigning the presidency of the bank, and, to use his own words, "felt like a school-boy off for his holidays." It had been a custom of his to go in swimming at North Beach, and he told me he was off for a swim, and he wanted me to go with him. I warned him that he was overheated, that the water of the Pacific was dangerously cold, and begged him to forego his bath; but he insisted. I was unable to go with him at the time, but promised if he would wait an hour I would go with him to North Beach. We then separated. I fully expected to find him waiting for me at the bath-house, but I was delayed, and the first thing I heard was the newsboys calling an extra with a statement of his suicide. The *Call* and the *Bulletin* had both been opponents of his, and were only too glad to do their dirty work. Mr. Ralston was a grand man, a noble man; he had no idea of suicide, and I so stated over my signature in the *Chronicle*. He was a courageous man, not a coward, was ready to meet all emergencies, and never discouraged. He was a friend of the poor man and the rich; he knew men, and his judgment never was at fault. His death was a great loss to the Pacific Coast, and Senator Sharon and the *Call* and the *Bulletin* were guilty of the foulest lie when they accused him of suicide. His death was due to cramp produced by his heated condition and very cold water.

Trusting these lines may be of some comfort from one who knows the facts, I am

Yours very sincerely,

JOHN PITMAN.

Ralston had one of the greatest civic imaginations in history, on a scale, as Miss Atherton notes, with such city-makers and castle-builders as Ludwig I and Ludwig II of Bavaria—both of whom almost built their state into bankruptcy. Ironically, most of Ralston's businesses, including the Bank of California, survived his death to make other stockholders rich. The hated Sharon went on to complete the Palace Hotel, which ranked as one of the world's greatest. Miss Atherton's words are Ralston's epitaph:

"He was a great man set down into too small a field, and, like other great men that have ignored the laws made by lesser men, he paid a heavy price."

The coronation of the new bonanza kings was greeted by holocaust. In a small wooden lodging house in Virginia City, an oil lamp tipped over on a dry October morning in 1875. The cracker-box building exploded in fire, and within minutes west winds carried the flames across the flimsy rooftops. At the south end of town, 500 wooden houses burned until three o'clock in the afternoon when the Washoe Zephyr set off a chain reaction of firestorms down C Street. Editor Dan De Quille described the city as "a sea of fire." The air was filled with cinders from rooftops which fluttered overhead like huge burning kites in the smoke. Church spires held flaming orange crosses in mile-high pillars of smoke, while the cries of children were drowned in a hideous tintinnabulation of fire sirens and bells.

John Mackay fell to his knees and cried out to God Almighty to save his mine. A million feet of lumber blazed outside the Con Virginia. Railroad car wheels were melted in the open air, and for thirty-six hours firemen poured water from hand engines down the shafts. As the million-dollar hoisting works blazed on the surface, Mackay made his ultimate deal with the Lord. If his shaft was spared, he would build twenty churches.

THE BONANZA KINGS:

Above: JOHN W. MACKAY

Below: JAMES C. FLOOD, WILLIAM S. O'BRIEN, JAMES G. FAIR

But it was not the God of Rome that saved Mackay's mine. Loyal muckers had dynamited the neighboring homes to form a rocky fireproof circle around the costly underground workings of the Con Virginia. Above ground, 2000 buildings were gone. Ten million dollars lost. Yet Virginia City, without a pause for nostalgia, rebuilt its charred guts in sixty days.

Incredibly, even as the town burned above him, Sutro bored into the mountain. The terrible problems of heat, of swelling clay and collapsing timbers, of ventilation and cave-ins intensified as he moved three, then four miles, to find a hookup with the Savage Mine shaft. His eight-by-twelve-foot shaft was creeping forward 350 feet per month as his Burleigh drills forced the header back into the rock-hard Comstock mineral belt.

The powder monkeys could not survive more than three hours in the stifling corridor, and crews were changed four times a day. Blasting into the precarious framing of the tunnel soon approached the delicate art of safecracking, and often the wooden timbers collapsed. And there was the constant problem of political obstruction.

As Sutro's mole men bored forward, the Irish muckers continued to dig headlong down into the mountain, toward the Hades of the 2000-foot level. Speculators in San Francisco guessed the Bonanza Kings were onto a new, deeper vein; they were wrong. While doing nothing to discourage such optimism, the Irishmen did everything to slow Sutro—even unto employing the bad offices of their former archenemy, now Senator William Sharon. The Bonanza Kings had extracted over $200 million from the earth, and while his partners continued to manipulate the frenzied market in Comstock securities John Mackay made good his vow to rebuild Virginia City in his own solid brick image.

The Kings had motives other than mere idle profit to stave off Sutro's tunnel. As fabulous as their fortunes in ore, they stood to make even more from the inflated value of their mining stocks buoyed to astronomical prices by the yet unpeaked speculation in San Francisco. But when Sutro's tunnel reached the deep shafts the true situation of the mines would be known outside the tight circle of the Bonanza King's superintendents.

Frenzied investors—touted by San Francisco harpies called "Mudhens" who hawked stocks on streetcorners like newspapers—were gambling that the deeper levels of exploration would yield new bonanzas—but no such strikes were forthcoming. The bonanza veins were nearing exhaustion. This the Kings knew but did not tell. Even as their stocks were rising the Irishmen were taking their profits out of mining and putting them into less spectacular but more secure investments. While Ralston had poured the Comstock's treasure into San Francisco as if the entire city were a silver mold, the Bonanza Kings spread their millions far and wide like distrustful spinsters not wishing to put all their eggs into one basket.

Sharon, the heir apparent to Ralston's empire, became a fading star in the western firmament, and after one last, losing battle with Sutro, he was defeated for reelection to the U.S. Senate by none other than James G. Fair, who outspent him. Upon his return to California, the white-haired ex-senator evicted Ralston's widow and family from Belmont and set up housekeeping in his dead friend's mansion. He was to spend his declining years indulging his penchant for petty feuds, but the tranquillity of his retirement was interrupted by a lawsuit from an attractive lady of mixed reputation, one Sarah Althea Hill, who claimed that Sharon had entered into a marriage contract with her and then defaulted after having reaped the benefits. During the scandalous litigation, Sharon died of a heart attack.

Four days after the Fourth of July, 1878, Adolph Sutro lighted a powder cartridge in the rocky upper wall of his four-mile tunnel, 1640 feet below Virginia City.

The charge blasted a jagged hole into the wall of the tunnel, and foul, burning air shot forward into the shafts and stopes of the adjoining Savage Mine. Pulverized rock whipped about the muckers as they pressed forward in the sulphurous darkness toward the flickering orange light of the great corridor below. The muckers shoved a ladder into the charred hole as a victory cannon boomed at the mouth of the tunnel 20,081 feet from the explosion. Adolph Sutro climbed up the ladder.

In late October 1879, former president Ulysses S. Grant, visiting the Comstock at the end of his world tour, led a spectacular victory procession through the Sutro Tunnel.

Hundreds of little mules, with candles on their collars, walked along the tracks pulling their masters in wagon cars, their ears twitching in cadence to the songs of the muckers and powder monkeys.

"The Star-Spangled Banner" echoed in the chamber over a rousing chorus of "When Johnny Comes Marching Home Again" and a thousand "Hurrah's" punctuated the unctuous strains of "In the Sweet Bye and Bye."

Along the four-mile tunnel, great elongated shadows of the procession flickered in a sepulchral rhythm to the great chorale. The official party and the attending dignitaries walked in solemn formation behind the retired Commander in Chief of the nation. Their long black coats were lost in shadow, and only the faces of the dignitaries were illuminated above their starched white collars by a mile-long column of candles.

Memories of the titanic struggle for the mountain, of the bonanza that lay embedded in its rock, welled up in powerful unspoken emotion in the hearts of the men who walked like monks through the catacombs of the Big Magnet.

The struggle was over, but few of them knew it.

The Irish four, having opened the Big Magnet to daylight, still kept their dark secret. The silver bonanza had petered out. Its giant vein had abruptly disappeared deep in the earth. For a few brief years the Bonanza Kings had stripped the world's biggest treasure chest in the cavernous underground chambers of the Con Virginia. They had their hands on the last bonanza ore as Sutro broke through to the Savage Mine. Soon the Kings would abdicate. The Irishmen would go on to bigger but not better things, to nearly corner the world wheat market, to lay the Atlantic cable, to build churches and colleges as monuments to their own mortality.

The procession reached its destination at the Savage Mine. H. T. P. Comstock's ghost must have laughed over the scene from some foul chamber in the earth. The one man who, by all worldly rights, should have marched with Grant at the head of the parade was not there.

Adolph Sutro was in disgrace, the talk of the town, the victim of scandal. His wife had caught him with a bird and a bottle in a private suite with a mysterious widow at the International Hotel. His own overdeveloped sense of Victorian morality had kept Sutro from accompanying the ex-President.

It was like a bad joke about a man who was absent from his own funeral. Only the funeral was that of the Comstock. Sutro, like the Irishmen, had discovered that the mountain would soon be barren, that his tunnel was a white elephant. And while the procession scattered out of the Savage Mine to the call of new and distant bonanzas, an embittered Sutro secretly sold out his personal stock in the Tunnel Company on the New York Exchange, becoming a millionaire at the expense of the miners who had supported him.

Adolph Sutro would wander in Europe, where the conscience-stricken visionary was to accumulate one of the world's great collections of books—a magnificent library for San Francisco. And in almost ritual atonement for his abandonment of the miners, he would beautify San Francisco as the environmentalist, populist mayor of the city that was built by silver from his Comstock Lode.

The echoes of the candlelit mule procession faded in the empty four-mile corridor under Sun Mountain. The richest place on earth rested, perhaps forever.

THE PARADE THAT PASSED SUTRO BY

Above:
VIRGINIA CITY—BEFORE THE FIRE OF 1875

Below:
AFTER THE FIRE

Overleaf:
LAST GREAT VIEW OF VIRGINIA CITY FROM THE EAST—
HIGH SIERRA IN THE DISTANCE

Triptych for Virginia City

❦

ELEGY AFTER THE FIRE

ALLEGORY FOR VIRGINIA CITY

TWENTIETH CENTURY VIRGINIA CITY

Epilogue

NIGHTS IN
VIRGINIA CITY

by Fredric Hobbs

It was 1947 when I rode in young Clyde Souter's '36 Ford up the Geiger Grade to Virginia City. As we careened over the summit, past a blur of red rock and pines, I sensed a strange quiet in the afterglow of the evening, a mood that I would later come to know as a curious nostalgia. I was going back into time, into a landscape bathed in rusty light, into a place that had lived in history.

We rounded the curve that hung like a great rocky balcony over the ghost mines and tailings of the Comstock Lode and I heard the distant plunks of a banjo. Then many banjos echoing over the mountains in the cool night air. Virginia City loomed up before us like a narrow corridor of light, a night version of El Greco's "View of Toledo" in close-up.

C Street, the main drag, was vaguely defined in a blue half-light from old street lamps and storefronts, and telephone poles grew in slanted abstraction to a vanishing point at the far end of town. The banjo chorus faded in and out from the weathered brick and wood buildings.

> Buffalo Gal, won't ya come out t'night, come
> out tonight, come out t'night,
> Buffalo Gal, won't ya come out t'night and
> dance by the light a the moon.

Young Clyde turned abruptly down D Street to a row of one-story houses that once overlooked John Mackay's Consolidated Virginia Mine. At the side road, windows cut holes in little tarpaper buildings, and, on the hill, rotting timbers held up the C Street buildings in dark relief against the mountain.

The D Street miners' shacks were whorehouses now, and the glowing windows framed bodies of women of all ages and in all manner of costume. Women with gold teeth smiled at us, beckoning to scared fifteen-year-olds through half-open doors. Others sat at cash registers or stared out the windows into Six Mile Cañon. But only the sheriff's headlights saved us from sin that night as we sped down the Geiger Grade to the comparative safety of Reno.

I next visited the Comstock in the fifties, as a young air force lieutenant driving over from Tahoe with college girls in their starched dresses. Tourists were on the mountain by the thousands now, and along the Geiger Grade, Virginia City billed itself as "THE LIVELIEST GHOST TOWN IN THE WEST." More than twenty saloons occupied historic buildings on C Street and, down the hill, the D Street whores had departed for air-conditioned trailers at the edge of Storey County.

The summer evening was alive with the cacophony of tourism. Creaking boardwalks were full of nervous laughter and silly talk, while in the saloons and restaurants endless waves of honky-tonk piano almost drowned out the steady low clank of slot machines.

> Ohh the moon shines tonight on pretty Red Wing,
> On pretty Red Wing, On prEEEty Red Wing . . .

One drink, two drinks, three drinks, four . . . Five drinks, six drinks, seven drinks more.

> OHHHHH, the moon shines tonight on PRETTY RED WING!

I grabbed my date and danced her across C Street through the high narrow door of the Union Brewery Saloon. The honky-tonk faded abruptly, and I felt like I had danced into church.

This saloon was not like the others.

I still cannot quite describe the Union Brewery, even after staggering in and out of it for the past twenty years. Maybe it's the light. At nine-thirty in the evening, the nasty old room takes on the soothing tones of a tawny lion's skin. Or maybe it's the booze they serve. Some concoctions that have been served there would melt the Grosch brothers' alchemical retorts. Or maybe it's the folks that amble in.

The Brewery is still good today, but it was great in the fifties, like a swell private club with no dues. Highway Harry, Keeper of the Grade, held up the end of the old bar, Garbage Mike sucked on his stained pipe and mumbled Basque parables through his beard, and Major the Dog kept discipline. Egloo, the mining historian, Walt with the laugh, Harry the piano player who looked like Lionel Barrymore, and Louie the French Cowboy, Editor Bob of the *Enterprise*, Senator McGirk, all observed the rules of the house. Even Lucius Beebe and Chuck Clegg dropped in. They were right out of the Comstock a hundred years ago. There were some great broads around the Comstock then, legitimate ladies who danced and applauded Jack Curran and the banjo band at Saturday night "mass." And it was not unusual for us regulars to demand encores from a spoon player who sat in with the banjos during dawn hours of the Sabbath.

Presiding over the ritual was Gordon Lane, proprietor of the Union Brewery Saloon. With ash blond hair parted squarely in the middle, he was the perfect vision of the town iconoclast, philosopher and king, a laughing one-man audience in his own house. Many times over the years I have sat in blurry conversation with my friend Gordon, after the banjos were silent, late after the last regular quit, and often, when there was nothing more to say, he left me to my dreams on the old church pew by the piano as he locked up for the night.

My night visions on Gordon's pew played like movies without words.

Rum boiled off, leaving voices. An unintelligible Greek Chorus whispered at me from behind a circle of bearded masks and I pulled back to focus on the scene. It was snowing in the saloon.

Whispers faded to the wind and the masks became bearded miners who danced an endless serpentine reel over a floor of snow. I was pulled into the ritual. I floated out through the open door, following the column of men into a stark mountain landscape. A lone man passed us, sliding down the mountainside on snowshoes in the opposite direction of the advancing column. But the column ignored him. The bearded men were intent on the ground before them as they shuffled in their antlike search for something blue and glowing, something beneath the mountain's skin. Something larger than themselves.

On the distant summit of the mountain, a jackass screamed into the wind. Its teeth bared electric blue, like irridescent jewels in the snow, and the ground melted to mud. It was the signal the men had waited for, and they broke ranks all over the rocky slopes, turning the great pyramid-mountain into a giant beehive.

I was to see more of this dream movie during the next decade. Nearly always I thought of it when I visited Gordon's, when the Greek Chorus laughed and danced and whispered around my head at night. I began to see the saloon band as a memory, always playing in a frenzied, speeded-up accompaniment to the action of my "movie." Away from Nevada, my daytime woolgathering became hallucinatory, an exercise in the surreal imagination. Now the banjo band wore jackass heads and their hands plucked metallic shrieks from the full moons of their instruments. I had a jackass band to back up my dancing, bearded Miner's Chorus, and it didn't much matter when I read the ravings of so-called historians and other reporters of the Comstock Era. Apparently the rocky, silver-hearted mountain made them crazy too.

In two decades the mountain had exploded. Its riches became legend. And everybody from Mark Twain to Baron Rothschild came to pay homage to it, to pat its shimmering belly. But others came to rape and plunder it and to carry off its treasures.

One day, not too long ago, I mused upon these heathen usurpers as I walked among the ruins of the mines near American Flats. I peered into the dark, abandoned stopes and the jackass band started up again. But the bearded Chorus was not laughing. The scene was more like a hideous underground ballet with choreography by Goya. Thousands of torsos, heads, and arms hurled themselves at rocks from within a giant honeycomb of wooden cages, and tiny black picks animated the walls like the inner workings of a terrible subterranean clock.

My eyes tilted slowly up the narrow shafts of light that led to the surface of the mountain. The noise was deafening. Silver machines were locked over every opening in the earth. Enormous wheels drove pestles into lead bowls in the center of clustered chimneys, and black and brown columns of smoke gushed forth into the lifeless yellow sky above the mines. This symphony of horrors was punctuated by the dull chug of a long silver train that wound like a metal choke on the mountain, where the column of men used to be.

I closed my eyes and got the hell out of there fast. The rape of the mountain was too depressing to watch, so I superimposed a subjective overhead hovering shot from a nineteenth-century observation balloon for another look at the Comstock. Things weren't much better in this scene either.

The famous banking titans and Irish bonanza kings were at a killing sport in an outdoor arena that resembled a big boxing ring. Around them sat a crowd of top-hatted men and fancy ladies with parasols eating sandwiches and drinking champagne.

At the edge of the crowd a small group of Indians stood watching. The Irishmen were winning. John Mackay was stripped to the waist and appeared to be fighting a frock-coated Ralston according to the rules of the Marquis of Queensborough. The fighting was all very civilized, until a little gray-haired man ran up behind Ralston and stabbed him between the shoulders with a long silver knife. As Ralston crumpled to the ground in the dust, the crowd applauded politely, like spectators at a tennis match. When I tried to follow the boxers into the crowd I lost them in an overlapping montage of historical trivia of what the bonanza millionaires did with their money, and the scene resolved into a sea of clapping hands.

Later, I thought of what had made the bearded Chorus and the bankers and Mark Twain and the Irishmen stick it out in this hole called Sun Mountain. They wanted more than money. And they were here for the same reason. They wanted to be near the greatest abstraction of wealth the world had ever seen, to gaze upon it, to bathe their souls in its faint luminous energy. To listen to its whispered promise of immortality.

There have been descriptions of the great underground chamber of silver and gold that was the Big Bonanza at the Consolidated Virginia Mine in the heart of the mountain, below Virginia City, but I preferred to step into the elevator shaft myself to see what it was like. In the fading light, my dream movie unfolded in my head.

I was sinking in a mine elevator into the underground chasm where I had last seen the pyramid of toiling bodies, the Goyaesque ballet. Faster until the dark walls blurred into an oscillating blue green glow. The Chorus of miners seemed far away, in a huge echo chamber, and as the elevator passed the lighted way stations on its downward course to the lower level, I sensed that I was in a strange vertical subway train to hell. Sparks spewed from the metal cage as it brushed against the quartz walls of the mine shaft, and for brief irregular moments the walls were illuminated like a flash fire of diamonds. Then cross drafts began to rock me in a violent semidarkness.

The elevator jolted to rest on a shimmering, translucent floor of silver. I pushed open the cage door and stumbled out into an enormous chamber. The walls stretched out before me as giant trapezoids, framed in timbers, soaring to a gothic pyramid of space. Burnished amber stalactites hung from the ceiling, and, at the end of the corridor, a monumental garnet altar cast its own light. I approached to touch the hypnotic presence of the surface.

The garnet rocks glowed like wine in old bottles. But they were ice to the touch. The silver slab under my feet numbed my body and almost at once I was frozen to the spot, my gaze riveted to the wall of garnet eyes in front of me. I was locked in fear, possessed by a deep, penetrating light force that was suspending me in time like an instant human fossil.

I raged at the curiosity that had brought me here, and I screamed terror at the petrification of my body. I was going blind and I begged for salvation and the chamber echoed my cries in a high-pitched wave of sound. Then I fell back sliding, without weight, as though a great magnet has released me.

The waves of sound faded back into the walls as I scrambled away from the altar. The ceiling warped about my tumbling body and the masks of the bearded miners' Chorus appeared in superimposition over the glowing rocks. The white masks of the Chorus floated toward me, muffling the final echoing sound. The great slab was quiet again and only the whispering masks followed my flight to the open door of the elevator.

I slammed the iron door and collapsed against the metal cage. The elevator lifted rapidly and, as the calming atmosphere of the upper levels began to revive me, the unholy apparition of the jackass from the mountain materialized in the corner of the cage. Its bony irridescent blue teeth grinned at me for a moment in the darkness and vanished. The banjos started up again and I was safe from the terrible vision and I knew I would wake up in Gordon's saloon.

When I surfaced from the dream, I knew the heart of the mountain, the abstraction of wealth that drove men crazy. The miners had braved holocaust to be near it and the bonanza titans had fought each other to the death for its riches. Perhaps Adolph Sutro, the Mad Prometheus of the Tunnel, had been the only man to understand its energy. But for me, the Big Magnet was a confrontation with the reality of death, the motivation behind the pyramids, the force that always builds great monuments to the mortality of man.

Virginia City
1977

Overleaf:
MINER ANGELS

Notes on
the Drawings

———◦———

Notes on
Historical Sources

Notes on the Drawings

Ingres, the French master, said that drawing is the probity of art, and, as one who has always approached drawing as a primary art form, I am inclined to agree with him.

For me, drawings are akin to chamber music, and the smaller the format, the more challenging the task of making a few black lines come alive on white paper. The true and worthy task, however, and one that is not currently in fashion, is to *see* form with line.

I have endeavored to make drawings—not illustrations—for *The Richest Place on Earth*. The experience rather than a picture of the experience. My background in cinema and my contributions to the text have influenced the continuity of the drawings, providing a kind of visual narrative to the story. At least that was the idea.

Many of the images, the iconography of the muckers, seem to jump off the pages at the viewer. To violate the sacred "picture plane" of the support—which in this case is a book—I composed them this way. Duelers are back to back along a line where the book is bound, and some of the larger-than-life characters scramble all over the surface of the page for air as if they had been suffocating too long in Sharon's mines of century past.

C. F. H.

Notes on Historical Sources

Some observations. Jacob Burckhardt in his monumental work on the Italian Renaissance tells of the leaders of a city trying to decide how to reward a general who had saved them from foreign peril. They concluded that no honor within their power to bestow was great enough. At last they decided to kill him and worship him as their patron saint.

There is a bit of that madness in the *historie* of Virginia City. The chroniclers of the Comstock seemed to have troubles deciding how to be nice enough to its heroes; one is hard put to find a villain, save for a sagebrush bandido or two. Even the outlaws are glory be'd—witness Slade, Mark Twain's "democratic hero-villain" with his "history-creating revolver" who was the ruler of a "very paradise of outlaws and desperadoes."

Everything about the Comstock seems to be exaggerated except its faults. Most biographies of its major figures range from the merely uncritical to exercises in hagiography. When on rare occasions it must be allowed that a great man has done a foul deed, the standard works on Virginia City tend toward the seventeenth-century practice of blaming the misconduct of rulers on evil counselors or ignoring the mischief entirely with the blitheness of the man who says "Girl? What Girl?" when his wife catches him in bed with another woman.

For example, in their 1962 biography *Adolph Sutro*, Robert E. and Mary Frances Stewart will not hear it that Sutro's secret unloading of his shares in the Sutro Tunnel before his friends found out the Lode had become as valuable as a wet graham cracker was anything less than angelic. A more realistic assessment of Sutro's action—and of the general knavery of the Comstock nabobs—is to be found in Gilman M. Ostrander's excellent 1966 history of the strangeness that is Nevada, *Nevada: The Great Rotten Borough, 1959–1964*. Oscar Lewis in his lively 1947 biography of Mackay, Fair, Flood, and O'Brien, *Silver Kings*, justly tars the Irish Four with the brush of monopoly and details for the curious reader the near hilarity of the follies of inherited wealth as the fortunes trickle downhill into the sewer of the twentieth cenury in a riot of contested wills, paternity suits, and motorcar crashes.

The authors in the present work while staying clear of the shoals of hagiography have attempted to avoid the rocks of moralism. Virginia City was the cradle of Western Wealth, which had been distinguished by an absence of New England gentility and Eastern pretense about being unconspicuous about consumption. Its story deserves to be told on its own terms as it is told here, without blinders, and without attempting to make an enlightened capitalist out of a worm like Senator Sharon, as many Comstock books do.

The history of Virginia City does little to validate Frederick Jackson Turner's overblown thesis about frontier democracy. It is actually more a Western Faust, where all the silver titans, the miners, and the lumpen of San Francisco all bit of the same apple of speculation and optimism and each made his own bargain with the devil. It was the richest place on earth for an enormous quarter century, and when it ended it ended with a thud, not a whimper. People made their pile and got out and never bothered to look back or blink an eyelash in sentimentality. "Poor man's pudding" was John Mackay's description of the Comstock after he left it. Virginia City had gone from paranoia to riot, carnage to intrigue, triumph to tragedy, to pudding.

For the reader who wishes to pursue further the roller coaster of Comstock lore, the best of the previous works on the Lode are conveniently available in Ballantine paperback editions in the Comstock Series of Western Americana. These would be the aforementioned *Silver Kings* by Oscar Lewis; Dan De Quille's classic of life in the mines and Comstock lore, *The Big Bonanza*, originally published in 1876 under Mark Twain's sponsorship; and two volumes of George Lyman's chatty and never-quite-finished history of the Comstock, *The Saga of the Comstock Lode* (1934) and *Ralston's Ring* (1937). Lyman, of all the Comstock writers, is the closest to the delightful historian George Dangerfield in his wit and pace, although he at times has difficulty distinguishing melodrama from drama.

The remainder of the works mentioned here that were consulted by the authors are either out of print or not readily available in most suburban public libraries. This list is not meant to be a complete bibliography of works on the Comstock nor does it represent the totality of the authors' own research, which included the files of early San Francisco newspapers and the extant records of the *Territorial Enterprise* and the *Evening Chronicle* of Virginia and the *Gold Hill News*.

One should be cautious in consulting the noble Hubert H. Bancroft's famous *Chronicles of the Builders* since the West's great men could do no wrong in Bancroft's sublimely mawkish view. Sam Davis' chronicle of Nevada, *History of Nevada* (1913), while not exactly the stuff of revisionism, has more amusing and intriguing material than Myron Angel's 1881 *History of Nevada*. (The modern reader would do well to first consult Ostrander's *Nevada: The Great Rotten Borough* mentioned above.) Of the original memoirs of life on the Comstock, Senator Stewart's *Reminiscences* (1908) are more about him than them; the dispatches of the brilliant artist-journalist, world traveler, and diplomat J. Ross Browne—who wrote for *Harper's Weekly* in the 1850s and '60s—are unmined jewels of description of Virginia City; and the veteran editor Wells Drury's *An Editor on the Comstock Lode* (1936) is a delight. Of course no one could begin to learn the West of the Silver Fever without Mark Twain's magnificent *Roughing It*, which, happily, is available in library and inexpensive editions alike.

The basic classic on the Comstock mines is Eliot Lord's *Comstock Mining and Miners* (1883), which has been reprinted in a fascimile edition by Howell-North of Berkeley (1959). Lord, who was without compeer on mining history, was a perfect ass about the motives and mechanizations of the mine owners. On the other hand, Charles Howard Shinn in his *The Story of the Mine* (1896) and his earlier work on the California mining camps stubbornly attempts to make the mines into a Nirvana of social experience.

Another exercise in telling the Comstock story, which has the virtue of capturing it all between two covers, is C. B. Glassock's *The Big Bonanza* (1934). There is also for the further seeker-after-fact an attempt at biography of the elusive Eilley Orrum by Swift Paine, *Eilley Orrum: Queen of the Comstock*, which is sort of a 1929 pseudo-novelistic exercise in psychohistory; a previously noted 1962 biography, *Adolph Sutro*, which while commendable errs on the wrong side of idolatry; and a recent (1975) biography of Ralston by David Lavender, *Nothing Seemed Impossible: William C. Ralston and Early San Francisco*, while heavy in scholarship leaves a strange taste from the author's apparent jealousy of his subject.

Of sources somewhat afield of Comstock center, the authors have been enlightened by Gertrude Atherton's graceful *California: An Intimate History* (1914); Franklin Walker's *San Francisco's Literary Frontier* (1939); Allen Weinstein's *Prelude to Populism: Origins of the Silver Issue, 1867–1878* (1970); Maxwell Geismar's *Mark Twain: An American Prophet* (1970), which is the best critical biography of Twain ever written and the only book that treats Twain as the radical, demonic social critic he was rather than the frontier humorist and fantasist his establishment biographers would paint him; and Kevin Starr's superlative *Americans and the California Dream* (1973).

Journalism buffs will delight in Lucius Beebe's *Comstock Commotion: The Story of the Territorial Enterprise* (1954), which also affords a grand overview of Comstock history. Beebe's *The Big Spenders* (1966) amusingly traces some of the Comstock silver fortunes on their eastward course, and all of Beebe and Charles Clegg's books on western railroading and history, which invariably touch on Virginia City, are fine reading.

Finally there is James M. Cain's novel *Past All Dishonor*, which draws more than metaphorically on the story of the Comstock Lode.

W. H.

About the Authors

Warren Hinckle III

WARREN HINCKLE is a fourth-generation San Franciscan whose grandmother was a dance-hall girl in the old Barbary Coast. At the Jesuit University of San Francisco, he was the prize-winning editor of the student newspaper, *The Foghorn*. He worked as a reporter for the San Francisco *Chronicle* before launching a publishing career as editor and president of *Ramparts* magazine during its famous muckraking years of the 1960s. In the seventies he has been a founder and editor of the controversial *Scanlan's Monthly*, which John Dean in his White House memoirs described as the magazine former president Richard Nixon hated most, and the editor of film director Francis Ford Coppola's experimental weekly *City of San Francisco*.

Hinckle received the Thomas Paine Award in 1967 for his work in exposing the CIA's infiltration into American domestic institutions. His journalistic activities have been honored for his "explosive revival of the great muckraking tradition" (George Polk Award).

In addition to *The Richest Place on Earth*, Hinckle is the author of *Guerrilla War in the USA* (1971), *The Ten-Second Jailbreak* (1973), which was made into the motion picture *Breakout* starring Charles Bronson, and an autobiography *If You Have a Lemon, Make Lemonade* (1974). In addition to his own publications he has written for *Playboy*, *Esquire*, the *Atlantic Monthly*, and the *New York Times*.

Hinckle lives in San Francisco with his wife and two daughters in a home that a politically conservative newsletter once described as a decaying Victorian mansion in an interracial and bisexual neighborhood. He is 38.

Fredric Hobbs

C. FREDRIC HOBBS was born December 30, 1931, in Philadelphia. He attended Menlo School in Menlo Park, California, and was graduated in 1953 from Cornell University with a B.A. in history. He attended Madrid's Academia de Belles Artes for advanced study and was Artist in Residence and tennis coach at the Stevenson School in Pebble Beach, California.

In 1961 Hobbs founded the San Francisco Art Center. From 1962 to 1963, he directed the fine arts program at the Academy of Art College in San Francisco and was Chairman of the Fine Arts Department at Lincoln University. Hobbs pioneered the concept of driveable "parade" sculpture and drove the first sculpture car "Sun Chariot" across the country. His second parade sculpture, "Trojan Horse," became the subject of a TV and educational film by the same name and is owned by the Museum of Modern Art and the Metropolitan Museum in New York City. Hobbs has written, produced, and directed four feature motion pictures: *Troika, Roseland, Alabama's Ghost,* and *God-Monster.*

Hobbs's next breakthrough in the arts was the creation of the first "energy sculpture," a mass art form known as Survival Art that combines soft technology and ecological and educational motivational exercises with fine art. An exhibition of eight animated sculptures premiered at the California Museum of Science and Industry in Los Angeles the summer of 1976. In the past two decades Hobbs has held eighteen one-man exhibitions on the continent and in New York, Houston, Los Angeles, and San Francisco.

Hobbs is president of The Madison-Hobbs Companies, Inc., a motion-picture production, publishing, and real-estate design and development company in San Francisco.